Puzzling Quality Puzzles

Also available from ASQ Quality Press

Creativity, Innovation, and Quality
Paul E. Plsek

Quality Problem Solving
Gerald F. Smith

Root Cause Analysis: A Tool for Total Quality Management
Paul F. Wilson, Larry D. Dell, and Gaylord F. Anderson

Mapping Work Processes
Dianne Galloway

Quality Quotes
Hélio Gomes

Let's Work Smarter, Not Harder: How to Engage Your Entire Organization in the Execution of Change
Michael Caravatta

The Change Agents' Handbook: A Survival Guide for Quality Improvement Champions
David W. Hutton

Understanding and Applying Value-Added Assessment: Eliminating Business Process Waste
William E. Trischler

To request a complimentary catalog of ASQ Quality Press publications, call 800-248-1946.

Puzzling Quality Puzzles

J.P. Russell and Janice Russell

ASQ Quality Press
Milwaukee, Wisconsin

Puzzling Quality Puzzles
J.P. Russell and Janice Russell

© 1998 by ASQ

All rights reserved. No part of this book may be reproduced in any form or by any means, electronic, mechanical, photocopying, recording, or otherwise, without the prior written permission of the publisher.

10 9 8 7 6 5 4 3

ISBN 0-87389-425-1

ASQ Mission: To facilitate continuous improvement and increase customer satisfaction by identifying, communicating, and promoting the use of quality principles, concepts, and technologies; and thereby be recognized throughout the world as the leading authority on, and champion for, quality.

Attention: Schools and Corporations
ASQ Quality Press books, videotapes, audiotapes, and software are available at quantity discounts with bulk purchases for business, educational, or instructional use. For information, please contact ASQ Quality Press at 800-248-1946, or write to ASQ Quality Press, P.O. Box 3005, Milwaukee, WI 53201-3005.

For a free copy of the ASQ Quality Press Publications Catalog, including ASQ membership information, call 800-248-1946.

Printed in the United States of America

 Printed on acid-free paper

Quality Press
611 East Wisconsin Avenue
Milwaukee, Wisconsin 53202

Contents

Preface xi
Introduction: How to Use This Book xiii
Acknowledgments xvii

Part 1: Quality Crossword Quotes 1
   1-1: Go to the Source 3
   1-2: Expense vs. Benefit 5
   1-3: The Struggle 7
   1-4: Anarchy 9
   1-5: The Success Duo 11
   1-6: Lost at Sea 13
   1-7: In a Class by Itself 15
   1-8: How Do We Get There? 17
   1-9: Molehills Not Mountains 19
   1-10: Mind and Matter 21
   1-11: The Magic of Discovery 23
   1-12: Mental Overload 25
   1-13: The Educated Eye 27
   1-14: The Key to It All 29
   1-15: "Make It So" (Captain Jean Luc Picard) 31
   1-16: Hit and Run 33

Part 2: Decipher the Words of the Coded Quality Quotes 35
   2-1: Just Reward 37
   2-2: Poor Vision 37
   2-3: Astounding! 39

2-4:	How's Your Aim?	39
2-5:	Make Change	41
2-6:	Prime Importance	41
2-7:	Oh to Joy!	43
2-8:	We Aim to Please	43
2-9:	Go for the High Road	45
2-10:	The Prevaricator's Tool	45
2-11:	A Word to the Wise	47
2-12:	What Makes It Tick?	47
2-13:	The Ugly!	49
2-14:	Look for the Silver Lining	49
2-15:	Well, I Reckon	51
2-16:	Pass the Word On	51

Part 3: Find the Quality Words 53

3-1:	In the Field	55
3-2:	Quality Business	57
3-3:	Planning the Audit	59
3-4:	Auditor	61
3-5:	The Stakeholder	63

Part 4: Discover the Quality Quote 65

4-1:	Continuous Improvement	67
4-2:	Tunnel Vision	69
4-3:	All Roads Lead to Rome	71
4-4:	Mountaintop Experience	73
4-5:	What Real Teams Do!	75
4-6:	Costs of Quality	77
4-7:	Cooperation	79
4-8:	What Tomorrow Brings	81

Part 5: Crazy Crosswords 83

5-1:	Crazy Quality Daffynitions	85
5-2:	Crazy Quality Daffynitions	87
5-3:	Crazy Quality Daffynitions	89
5-4:	Crazy Quality Daffynitions	91
5-5:	Crazy Quality Daffynitions	93

Part 6: Quality Anecdotes 95
- 6-1: Fly-By-Night 97
- 6-2: Ask the Customer 99
- 6-3: Making Impressions 101
- 6-4: Moving Target.. 103
- 6-5: Shipping Gone Haywire 105
- 6-6: Monopoly Potholes in Customer Service 107
- 6-7: Making Suggestions 109
- 6-8: Handling a Complaint................................... 111
- 6-9: Quality First... 113
- 6-10: Regrade for Quality 115

Part 7: Find the Missing Word of the Quality Quote ... 117
- 7-1: Living in the Past...................................... 119
- 7-2: Top Down.. 121
- 7-3: Bottom Line 123
- 7-4: Problem Solved.. 125
- 7-5: Majority of One.. 127
- 7-6: Whose Job Is It Anyway? 129
- 7-7: What's Happening? 131
- 7-8: "I Love Ya' Tomorrow" (Annie) 133
- 7-9: Train to Nowhere! 135
- 7-10: What's for Dessert? 137

Final Puzzle: Stands Alone 139

Answer Section 141
- 1-1: Go to the Source....................................... 143
- 1-2: Expense vs. Benefit 144
- 1-3: The Struggle... 144
- 1-4: Anarchy 145
- 1-5: The Success Duo 145
- 1-6: Lost at Sea 146
- 1-7: In a Class by Itself.................................... 146
- 1-8: How Do We Get There? 147
- 1-9: Molehills Not Mountains............................... 147
- 1-10: Mind and Matter...................................... 148

1-11:	The Magic of Discovery	148
1-12:	Mental Overload	149
1-13:	The Educated Eye	149
1-14:	The Key to It All	150
1-15:	"Make It So" (Captain Jean Luc Picard)	150
1-16:	Hit and Run	151
2-1:	Just Reward	153
2-2:	Poor Vision	153
2-3:	Astounding!	153
2-4:	How's Your Aim?	153
2-5:	Make Change	153
2-6:	Prime Importance	153
2-7:	Oh to Joy!	153
2-8:	We Aim to Please	153
2-9:	Go for the High Road	153
2-10:	The Prevaricator's Tool	154
2-11:	A Word to the Wise	154
2-12:	What Makes It Tick?	154
2-13:	The Ugly!	154
2-14:	Look for the Silver Lining	154
2-15:	Well, I Reckon	154
2-16:	Pass the Word On	154
3-1:	In the Field	155
3-2:	Quality Business	156
3-3:	Planning the Audit	157
3-4:	Auditor	158
3-5:	The Stakeholder	159
4-1:	Continuous Improvement	161
4-2:	Tunnel Vision	162
4-3:	All Roads Lead to Rome	163
4-4:	Mountaintop Experience	164
4-5:	What Real Teams Do!	165
4-6:	Costs of Quality	166
4-7:	Cooperation	167
4-8:	What Tomorrow Brings	168
5-1:	Crazy Quality Daffynitions	169
5-2:	Crazy Quality Daffynitions	169

5-3:	Crazy Quality Daffynitions	170
5-4:	Crazy Quality Daffynitions	170
5-5:	Crazy Quality Daffynitions	171
6-1:	Fly-By-Night	173
6-2:	Ask the Customer	173
6-3:	Making Impressions	174
6-4:	Moving Target	174
6-5:	Shipping Gone Haywire	176
6-6:	Monopoly Potholes in Customer Service	176
6-7:	Making Suggestions	177
6-8:	Handling a Complaint	178
6-9:	Quality First	179
6-10:	Regrade for Quality	179
7-1:	Living in the Past	181
7-2:	Top Down	182
7-3:	Bottom Line	183
7-4:	Problem Solved	184
7-5:	Majority of One!	185
7-6:	Whose Job Is It Anyway?	186
7-7:	What's Happening?	187
7-8:	"I Love Ya' Tomorrow" (Annie)	188
7-9:	Train to Nowhere!	189
7-10:	What's for Dessert?	190
	Final Puzzle: Stands Alone	191

Source Reference List 193

Preface

This book is designed for people who work in the quality field—quality trainers and people interested in quality improvement. It can be used for your own enjoyment, for those "in-between and waiting times," as a training aid in a formal classroom, or to pass around the office to make a point. These are basic word puzzles with a new twist: They are built around quality quotes and fundamental quality principles using quality terminology.

The idea of quality-focused puzzles came about when JP (ever practicing continuous improvement) was looking for ways to increase awareness and stimulate creative thinking in his classes. (How many times can you show the picture of the old woman/young lady to create an effect?) He found that puzzles are a fun icebreaker, and he even assigned them as homework. Participants enjoyed the novelty of having puzzles related to their field—and getting together to discuss the answers.

From childhood on, we have counted on words to live by: words that are inspirational when we are down, motivating when we need that extra push, affirming our ideas and belief systems, or jarring open the doors of creativity—words that provide the perfect phrase at the perfect time. The idea of creating word puzzles using quality quotes as well as quality terminology and situations was the combination of two loves—using words to live by and puzzles. Jan has always loved to do crosswords and other puzzles—especially since hearing that those who do them are less likely to become senile—so she starts the day with a cup of coffee and a puzzle (and yes, she does them in ink).

Some of us exhibit the symptoms of being "brain dead" from time to time. One remedy is to take a break or divert your attention to another issue. We have found that working on a crossword puzzle is an excellent way to get the creative juices flowing again. We believe that working this collection of puzzles will be a lot more fun than asking yourself how many things you could do with coat hangers, plastic bottles, or Styrofoam cups. Filling in the blocks of the puzzle even seems to have some therapeutic value of restoring order in a chaotic world.

JP also thought that quality professionals would enjoy crossword puzzles that relate to their field—as compared to the everyday crossword puzzle that queries readers about rivers in Russia or who won the 1942 Olympic shotput. So, it is our hope that you enjoy this book and that it causes you to stretch your imagination, gets your creative juices flowing, and restores a sense of order to your everyday stress-filled life.

Introduction: How to Use This Book

Puzzling Quality Puzzles consists of a number of word puzzles and anecdotal short stories with a quality theme. Individuals can use the puzzles and short stories to test their wits and knowledge, or to just have fun. Trainers can use them to liven up a presentation, as short attention-grabbers—especially after lunch when postprandial narcolepsy (sleepiness after eating) sets in—to make a point, or as team-building exercises.

The titles of the puzzles throughout the book relate to the specific topics on which they are based and, in some cases, provide a hint that will help you solve them. The crossword puzzles have a limited number of crossed words because the puzzle construction is limited to the words in each selected quality quote.

The book consists of a number of different types of word puzzles, including

- Part 1: Quality Crossword Quotes (find the quality quote in the crossword matrix)

    This is a series of crossword puzzles created from quality quotes. Each puzzle is really two puzzles in one. First, you are asked to fill in the crossword and then to come up with the quality quote. Solving the quote is much more difficult, so we have provided some words to help give you a start.

- Part 2: Coded Quality Quotes (test your ability to decipher encrypted codes)

    If you like to figure out codes, you will find this an excellent part of the book. It is straightforward: By simply deciphering the code you come up with the quality quote. We have provided 12 helpful hints, to help you solve the code, that you will not find in other puzzle books. Trainers can refer to the reference guide to identify a particular quote they might like to use to make a point in a class or presentation.

- Part 3: Find the Quality Words (you will recognize the known quality lingo)

  These puzzles require you to find words in a matrix of letters. Grouped according to the title, there are 36 to 44 terms to find in each puzzle. In training, you may want the participants first to solve the word matrix and then to discuss some of the terms that they found.

- Part 4: Discover the Quality Quote (find the quality quote in the letter matrix)

  This section can be compared to a quality quote treasure hunt. You are given a famous quality quote, and to solve this puzzle, you must find and circle the words of the quote located in the letter matrix. These puzzles are especially good for those in-between times such as waiting in airports, on airplanes, or in hotels, or as a mental massage. Trainers can use them for student homework, as icebreakers when participants share answers, or as a gentle antidote for that postprandial narcolepsy.

- Part 5: Crazy Crosswords (stretch your imagination to find the double meanings)

  These are standard quality terms with very unusual meanings attached to them. The word clues make you think twice, since they use quality terms but are not related to the quality field. We provide a list of the quality terms used in the puzzles at the beginning of the section to help make the link between the daffynition and the quality word easier. Individuals could use these to help stretch the imagination (for those "brain dead" times) and just for fun. Trainers could use this as an enjoyable class workshop to break up the monotony of some of the quality discussions or as an exercise (with tongue-in-cheek meanings) to emphasize the difference in usage of real quality terminology and the need for everyone to speak the same quality lingo.

- Part 6: Quality Anecdotes (short stories with a message)

   There are 10 short stories that pose situations that you must analyze and/or respond to. The focus of each short story is listed at the beginning of the part. These mini case studies are excellent training tools.

- Part 7: Find the Missing Word of the Quality Quote (find the quote and identify what is missing).

   This is a step-up level from Part 4. You are provided the quality quote, with all the words in the letter matrix except one. To solve the puzzle, you must search for the words of the quality quote and then deduce the missing one. For individuals, the treasure hunt becomes more challenging. For trainers, this is a good team-building exercise requiring group cooperation.

- The Final Puzzle is a favorite quality quote. It is both startling and awe-inspiring, and, it makes one think about today's and tomorrow's realities.

In summary, these word games will require you to use your imagination as well as express your knowledge; they are a printed version of the "executive's toy." They can be used on planes, in airports, in hotels, or while waiting for someone. They can fill those 5 to 10 minute times that are "in between." They may be used as icebreakers in training session, as a class activity to emphasize a specific learning, or just as mental massages—an improvement over solitaire.

Again, we hope that you relax and have fun with these puzzles and find many good uses for them in your personal and professional life!

Acknowledgments

I have been reared with "words to live by" (e.g. "All that you do, do with your might for things done by halves are never done right," "to begin, that's the hard part," etc.), and for those, I thank my mother, Eunice Peterson. I would also like to thank our son, Paul Russell who, at the point when all words starting running together, came through with some fine editing. Thanks, also, to JP for his infinite patience, and to my neighbor, Sharon Rutland, who always came through with a hug and a glass of wine when the going got tough.

Most of all, however, I would like to thank Helio Gomez for putting together his wonderful book, *Quality Quotes* (ASQ Press 1997), which became the inspiration and the ultimate resource for this book.

—Jan

I would like to acknowledge Jan for her cooperative spirit, puzzle contributions, and understanding for making this collective work possible. I also appreciate the thoughtful comments made by ASQ reviewers to help us improve the book during development. And last, thanks to Quality Press for their willingness to try a different kind of quality-related book.

—JP

PART 1

Quality Crossword Quotes

Each of the following crossword puzzles contains a famous quality quote and, in some cases, the author's name or part of the name, or the publication in which the quote appeared. To solve the puzzle, fill in the words of the numbered crossword matrix derived from the clues given, then arrange your words to form the quote. Clues are taken from the quality field and from everyday life and times (to lighten things up). Clues are also taken from titles of quality books, when small words are needed. If a word is repeated in the quote, it will be repeated in the clues given and therefore in the grid. The exact number of words, their arrangement, and punctuation, are set up in the blanks below the grid and clues.

The following 10 words are provided as helpful hints for solving the quality quote: "a, an, and, at, for, from, of, the, to, toward."

1-1

Go to the Source

ACROSS

4. Ability to get results
7. ___ of the Crisis (W. Edwards Deming)
8. ___ smarter not harder
9. Critical examination or board preceder
11. With "ing," a nonconformity
13. Toward
15. The human elements of quality
16. Puts things together
17. Big or small/mistrusted by liberals
18. ___ Best on Quality (Quality Press)

DOWN

1. Ivy league school
2. Interview question
3. ___ Circles
4. ___ based techniques
5. Often follows "how"
6. Interview starter
10. Add value
12. Plan ___ Check, Act! (Shewhart's Cycle)
14. ___ Quality Audit Handbook (Quality Press)
16. Request

Fill in your answer:

To _____ _____ _____ to _____ _____ , _____ ,

and _____ , _____ the _____ _____ _____

the _____ .

— _____ _____ _____ .

1-2

Expense vs. Benefit

ACROSS

2. *Principles ____ Quality Costs* (Quality Press)
3. Differences due to normal fluctuations
6. Vampire player Vincent ____
10. Peters' goal
11. The ____ of quality
13. Precedes vowels
15. ____ no time
16. "____ *Change Agents' Handbook*" (Quality Press)
17. Crosby says it's free
18. ____ apple a day keeps . . .
19. ____ *Sales Quality Audit* (George A. Smith, Jr.)

DOWN

1. Kind of panel
4. Tolerable
5. "____ nothing sacred?"
7. Within limits
8. Stars/stripes joiner
9. A circle measurement
12. ASQ's Body ____ Knowledge
14. ____ any price

Fill in your answer:

_____ _____ the _____ of _____ at an _____ _____

and the _____ of _____ at an _____ _____ .

—Robert A. Broh

1-3

The Struggle

Note: The clues in this puzzle were taken from "Show Biz."

ACROSS

1. "Out _____ Africa"
4. "High _____" (Grace Kelly)
6. Command _____ (for the Queen)
10. Actress Ava _____
11. "In _____ ence Day"
13. "_____ There " (Andy Williams)
15. Seeking perfection
17. "Once _____ a Mattress"

DOWN

2. "With every _____ of my being"
3. 50s Singing Group, The Bel _____ s
5. _____ Studios (Hollywood)
6. In "Dracula, "_____ evil (spreading throughout)
7. TV's "Days of _____ Lives"
8. "_____ View to Kill"
9. "Bonnie _____ Clyde"
12. "A Man _____ All Seasons"
14. "_____ Graduate"
16. "The _____ , the Bad, and the Ugly"

Fill in your answer:

The _____ and _____ of _____ _____ _____ _____

a _____ , _____ _____ _____ for _____ _____ .

—John W. _____

1-4

Anarchy

ACROSS

2. *At ____ Service Quality Frontier* (Quality Press)
5. Plan, ____, check, act! (Shewhart's Cycle)
7. *Lessons ____ Team Leaders* (Quality Press)
8. Toward
9. Not needed
12. Not agreeing to
14. *____ Quality Toolbox* (Quality Press)
15. *Out of ____ Crisis* (W. Edwards Deming)

DOWN

1. Selected
3. Unknown one
4. Cluster of people (e.g., management ____)
6. Nick ____ time
10. It may be ad hoc
11. Smallest article
12. ____ for use (out of spec)
13. *Quality ____ Still Free* (Philip Crosby)

Fill in your answer:

A _____ _____ a _____ of the _____ _____ from

the _____ to _____ the _____ .

— _____

1-5

The Success Duo (Jan's Favorite)

ACROSS
4. Used before audit, control, or policy
7. _____ control and capable
8. Weakest or missing _____
9. *After _____ Quality Audit* (Quality Press)
11. Fro's opposite
12. Exist
13. A gear
15. One of the authors of this book

DOWN
1. The human ingredient in quality
2. Goal of all businesses
3. Plant, car, or turn of the _____
5. Minus 4 blackbirds in a pie
6. Linkage word
10. Kinds of organs
14. _____ *Quality Audit Handbook* (Quality Press)

Fill in your answer:

_____ and _____ _____ the _____ _____ to

_____ _____ the _____ _____ _____ .

—J. P. _____

11

Lost at Sea

ACROSS
1. You and I
5. Apathy
6. Unkempt
9. Possess
11. ISO and ANSI
13. ASQ's Body ____ Knowledge

DOWN
2. Peters' quest
3. Falling ____ (going overboard)
4. "Prince ____ Tides" (Streisand)
5. What no men are . . .
7. "I ____ tell a lie"
8. Red or Black
10. Smallest article
12. A workbook term used with "how"

Fill in your answer:

_____ _____ _____ _____ of _____ _____

a _____ of _____ _____ to _____ .

—John W. Gardner

1-7

In a Class by Itself

Note: The clues to this puzzle were taken from arts and entertainment (literature, music, sports, movies).

ACROSS

3. Denotes international recognition in sports
5. "_____ Tomorrow Comes"
6. "Ordinary _____"
7. Bob, Carol, Ted, Alice joiner
9. Athletes endorse these
11. Beginnings in tennis
13. "Only _____" (Platters)

DOWN

1. The Rogers who liked all men
2. Synonym for royalties
3. Elite in sports recognition (see 3 across)
4. A film producer's goal: To _____ profits
7. "They _____ Ran"
8. Trophies or awards denote _____
10. "You've Gotta _____ Heart"
12. "I'm in Love with _____"

Fill in your answer:

_____ _____ _____ _____ _____

_____ , _____ , and _____ , _____ _____ _____

_____ _____ _____ _____ .

—V. Daniel Hunt

1-8

How Do We Get There?

ACROSS
3. The "J" in J.I.T
6. Fastened or brought about
9. Valentine's plea "_____ mine"
10. Sales term used to get products out
11. Working smarter not _____
12. Recent (as a just-added product)
13. Doing its job
14. Time or tense
15. Lot _____ lot inspection
16. *Juran On Quality _____ Design* (J. M. Juran)

DOWN
1. Political satirist Mark _____
2. Word often preceding end
4. Applied science
5. Joiner in Hamlet's query
7. Political runs
8. "I _____ tell a lie"
15. Step _____ step process

Fill in your answer:

_____ _____ _____ _____ _____ _____

_____ , _____ _____ _____ _____ , _____

_____ _____ _____ _____ .

—J. P. _____

1-9

Molehills Not Mountains

ACROSS

1. Meet face to face
6. Rather
7. Report or solve them
10. None's antithesis
11. The "U" in Quality
12. Partner with "then"

DOWN

2. *Principles* ____ *Quality Costs* (Quality Press)
3. Him and her
4. Him and her revisited
5. Humoring
8. Evolve
9. Of lesser size

Fill in your answer:

_____ _____ _____ _____ _____ , _____ of

_____ _____ , _____ _____ _____ .

—William S. Halsey

1-10

Mind and Matter

ACROSS
2. Upon
5. Guidance into the 21st century
7. Relies
8. *Juran ____ Quality by Design* (J. M. Juran)
9. Precedes manual or audit

DOWN
1. ____quality practices
3. Too
4. Counts on
6. The "E" in CEO
7. Information
10. "I'll know ____ when I see ____" (John Guaspari)

Fill in your answer:

_____ _____ _____ _____ _____._____

_____ _____ _____ _____ _____.

—Juran Institute, Inc.

1-11

The Magic of Discovery

ACROSS

1. _____ *Quality Toolbox* (Quality Press)
3. Unique persons
6. Frontliner in industry
7. *The Way _____ Strategy* (Quality Press)
8. Have
9. Find
12. Opposite of real (as in _____ losses)

DOWN

1. Possessive plural pronoun
2. Either it _____ or it isn't (compliance)
3. Participation (heavy duty in quality)
4. Permits
5. David Copperfield's field
10. "I'll know _____ when I see _____" (John Guaspari)
11. Neither this nor _____
13. _____ do list (job jar word)

Fill in your answer:

The _____ of _____ _____ _____ _____ _____

_____ _____ to _____ _____ _____ _____ _____ .

—Philip Caldwell

Mental Overload

ACROSS

1. Made in the USA
4. Largest
7. ____ much of a good thing
8. Often preceded by too or not
10. Data
13. Possess

DOWN

2. Superlative of some
3. Opposite of isn't
4. Big or small/mistrusted by liberals
5. Now
6. Neither this nor ____
8. Upper or middle (plural)
9. ____ solving techniques
11. Confronting
12. ____ *Quality Audit* (Quality Press)

Fill in your answer:

The _____ _____ _____ _____ _____ _____

_____ _____ _____ _____ _____ _____

_____ _____ .

—Lee Iacocca

1-13

The Educated Eye

ACROSS
4. *ISO 9000 and ____ Service Sector* (Quality Press)
5. Opinion
7. Oft-used article
8. Halloween trick prevention
9. Tracing is getting ____ here to there
10. The "S" of SQC
13. Statistical process control ____
14. Talent or knack
16. Larger ____ life

DOWN
1. ____ of the heart (affairs)
2. *At ____ Service Quality Frontier* (Quality Press)
3. Comparative of some
6. Deserves high priority
11. One of a kind
12. Fro's opposite
15. *Quality ____ Personal* (Harry Roberts)

Fill in your answer:

The ____ to ____ ____ from the ____ ____

____ ____ ____ ____ the ____ ____ .

—Hitoshi Kume

1-14

The Key to It All

ACROSS

4. Owns
5. Under ____ gun
6. Often used with even or al ____
9. Who are always right
12. Quality is about measuring ____
13. ____ *Quality Audit Handbook* (Quality Press)
15. Prefix with thing or one
16. Word used with 8 down or a sail
17. Suffix with straw or rasp
18. A button to start the pump

DOWN

1. Item of value
2. He and she
3. Deserves high priority
7. ____ we having fun yet?
8. A goal of accountants and aerialists
9. Business
10. Superlative of some
11. ____ even think about it!
14. Level or ____ distribution
16. Demonstrate

Fill in your answer:

_____ _____ the _____ _____ _____ _____

_____ _____ , _____ _____ _____ _____

_____ _____ _____ the _____ _____ _____ .

—Thomas _____

"Make It So" (Captain Jean Luc Picard)

ACROSS

5. Management auditing is a ____ idea
7. Neither this nor ____
8. Manufactured
9. Gait or rate
11. Required
12. Start of a valentine request

DOWN

1. An increase in value
2. Deming's: "Never ending ____"
3. Mandates
4. In workbooks used with "how"
6. Bring to a successful result
10. ____ home in any land

Fill in your answer:

To _____ _____ at a _____ _____ , _____ _____

_____ _____ _____ _____ .

—J. M. Juran

1-16

Hit and Run

Fill in the blanks (Note: Since this is a really difficult quote to put together and the subject is rather serious, the clues are intentionally easy. Hats off to you!)

ACROSS

1. Neither _____ nor that
3. Coke _____ it!
6. "Boy on _____ Dolphin"
7. "_____ Here to Eternity"
8. "_____ Like a Man" (60s song)
11. "_____ a change"
12. "Up, up, and _____!"
13. "Everybody's doing _____"
14. "_____ night, sweet prince"
15. _____ or less
16. Believe it or _____
18. I would if I _____

DOWN

1. Larger _____ life
2. "_____ unto the day is the evil thereof
4. Part of the problem or . . . the _____
5. To _____ list (job jar word)
9. Actor Kurt _____
10. Above all do no _____
12. _____ so to bed
17. Here's _____ you

Fill in your answer:

_____ _____ _____ _____ to _____ a _____

and _____ _____ _____ _____ . _____ _____

_____ _____ _____ _____ _____ .

—J. P. _____ and Terry Regel

PART 2

Decipher the Words of the Coded Quality Quotes

The following are coded quotes concerning some aspect or perception of quality. Some of the quotes are well known, others are from sages of the past. To decode the quotes, simply replace the coded letter with the correct letter. For example the word "mission" may be "lzuuzrt" with the "l" representing the "m," the "z" representing the "i," and so on. In each of the different puzzles, the code for the letters will be different.

Helpful Hints!

1. Single letters are either the article A or pronoun I.
2. Watch for contractions (words with apostrophes), which end in T D LD NT S VE LL.
3. Look for word endings (e.g., ious, ing, ally, ation).
4. Keep in mind that some letters almost never end words (e.g., A, B, I, J, Q, V, Z).
5. Look for THE and TH combinations (e.g., they, than, this, that, thing, etc.).
6. Start with small words (e.g., one to three letters).
7. Double letters can be EE, OO, LL, RR, FF, SS, etc. (e.g., good, need, business).
8. Look for the length of the word and letter placement.
9. Be aware of repeated letters (e.g., always, people, high, that).

10. After commas, look for conjunctive words (e.g., and, but, not, for, yet, so, etc.).

11. Sometimes, starting at the author's name will be easier, especially with anonymous, anon., Cicero, Goethe, George, Berry, etc.

12. Remember that you are putting together a sentence. If the words don't go together as in a sentence, then rethink.

2-1
Just Reward

TB WSA LS UINY WSA'GR NHUNWV
LSCR WSA'HH PRY UINY WSA'GR
NHUNWV PSYYRC.
—NCSCWFSAV

Additional Work Space:

2-2
Poor Vision

SF SRO'F FLIF FLUX HIO'F RUU FLU
RWPAFSWO. SF SR FLIF FLUX HIO'F
RUU FLU GMWNPUQ.
—C. T. HLURFUMFWO

Additional Work Space:

2-3

Astounding!

WO DP INN EWE GRP GRWLBV DP
IMP YIAITNP UO EUWLB, DP DUZNE
NWGPMINNX IVGUZLE UZMVPNQPV.
—GRUCIV PEWVUL

Additional Work Space:

2-4

How's Your Aim?

AN CLR AP IARFO IC ISMCZASW, AC
AP IARFO IC JASSASW ISO BFFGASW
XTPCDRFQP.
—CZDRIP YFQQM

Additional Work Space:

2-5

Make Change

NZ POLTFC NR UE EPPIH, NU GIRU
PEGC LWEIU UOHEIFO OLHM XEHD
XNUONT UOC EHFLTNQLUNET NURCVZ.
—FEHMET VNBBNUU

Additional Work Space:

2-6

Prime Importance

OR OD RWN AOPDR MA SEE UPMKENHD
AMP S HSV RM AOVQ CWSR GOVQ
MA CMPG WN OD RM QM OV RWOD
BVOXNPDN.
—RWMHSD FSPEZEN

Additional Work Space:

2-7

Oh to Joy!

DF DM T PVB FV RTSO FRO XOIOLDF
VL ZRTF DM EVVQ, DF DM T EUOTFOU
VIO FV OACOUDOIKO ZRTF DM XOFFOU.
—EVOFRO

Additional Work Space:

2-8

We Aim to Please

NOCN KVREOJP LDRTF SEDRFOTC
HVFJILDAF TIJ GVFJ SAIJDHJOTC JNDL
ZAIL RTTIPRTHDF.
—QRXOQ CRAXOT

Additional Work Space:

2-9
Go for the High Road

STF CHGY FIM KHTAYLYPF NSTC CI GSUY S AWSTZY, CWY XHLKC CWHTZ FIM GMKC QI HK CI LSHKY FIML KCSTQSLQK.
—STCWITF LIDDHTK

Additional Work Space:

2-10
The Prevaricator's Tool

DQSTS GTS DQTSS PFYHW KU JFSW: JFSW, HGCY JFSW, GYH WDGDFWDFNW.
—CGTP DZGFY

Additional Work Space:

2-11

A Word to the Wise

BDSUKURARGRCH   LRDCVG   GMC   VSILNVG
SJ   GMC   TRHC   EKI.
—VRVCDS

Additional Work Space:

2-12

What Makes It Tick?

TLUW   GF   QZVUJ   FZ   VMYGWI   FLU
DXMQU   KCW,   VZFGAMFGZW   GJ
UAUKPFLGWI.
—XUU   GMQZQQM

Additional Work Space:

2-13
The Ugly!

COR   PNIAC   COSTM   B   HRIANT   LBT   FN
SA   CN   SMTNIR   NI   LNXRI   ZH   B
HINDQRV.
—VBABBES   SVBS

Additional Work Space:

2-14
Look for the Silver Lining

ME   RCNOSOLN   LAAL   ME   RCCRTNQEONP
OE   AXATP   DMJMSONP;   M   CALLOSOLN
LAAL   M   DMJMSONP   OE   AXATP
RCCRTNQEONP.
—MEREPSRQL

Additional Work Space:

2-15

Well, I Reckon

PE PD PS FNSNIZJ BQIN KIQCPEZMJN
EQ INXAQS VK QVI YNCNXED ELZS EQ
MQZDE QC QVI ZEEZPSBNSE.
—ELQBZD XZIJUJN

Additional Work Space:

2-16

Pass the Word On

FTR NOLP SITSMI SKOGCGLX PT TPQIKC
OJTRP TNLGLX FTRK SKTVRHP TK
CIKYGHI, LTP WRCP HTESMOGLGLX.
—NGMMGOE CHQIKZILJOHQ

Additional Work Space:

PART 3

Find the Quality Words

The next set of puzzles have hidden quality words (quality lingo) in them. The words are listed below the matix. The hidden words go in all directions: up, down, backward, forward, and diagonally upward and backward. Circle the entire word even though many letters are used more than once and sometimes words overlap each other.

The words are grouped according to title, although there will be some words that are used in more than one puzzle. (For example, those mostly pertaining to auditing per se will be under "Auditor.")

There may be some words in the grid that are not listed in the columns below and therefore are not important.

3-1

In the Field

```
V  N  N  O  I  T  A  C  I  F  I  C  E  P  S
A  G  I  R  L  E  H  B  I  A  T  O  N  L  S
L  I  A  E  O  E  R  N  U  C  E  S  I  A  A
U  S  R  Z  C  A  D  R  Y  T  M  T  L  N  L
E  E  T  K  N  I  P  R  O  C  E  D  U  R  E
A  D  N  G  N  R  D  Q  F  R  I  E  Z  I  S
D  E  E  G  O  E  G  U  I  D  E  L  I  N  E
D  T  M  D  F  O  R  A  E  E  C  L  O  S  E
E  E  U  E  F  A  I  L  L  S  C  O  O  P  Y
D  C  C  F  I  E  C  I  D  E  A  A  L  E  T
T  T  O  A  S  Y  S  T  E  M  S  A  R  C  S
I  N  D  U  S  T  R  Y  E  I  N  R  A  T  E
G  O  A  L  U  U  L  O  R  T  N  O  C  A  T
H  C  T  T  E  F  U  N  C  T  I  O  N  E  A
T  C  A  E  R  F  L  O  W  D  E  T  A  I  L
```

Cause	Detail	Goal	Policy	Size
Check	Detect	Guideline	Procedure	Specification
Close	Document	Industry	Product	System
Control	Fact	Inspect	Quality	Test
Cost	Fail	Issue	Range	Time
Data	Field	Item	Rate	Trace
Default	Finding	Line	React	Train
Defect	Flow	Plan	Root	Value added
Design	Function	Plant	Sales	Zero

3-2

Quality Business

```
T E R A P W D R A D N A T S
F I S H B O N E C Y C L E S
D E D D A R V C E M A I L Q
W O R K M L A I R S E M I T
S T R U N D L V U I O N C E
E T H T T C U R S T S O C H
L R O C I L E E A P A R T Y
C B O U C A U S E H P A R G
R E P D I S O C M E A N S T
I N E O E S T E A M W O R K
C C R R G I S S E C O R P C
Y H A P O F F L E G N A R A
T M T N A G M E N I L O I B
I A I D L E L A C S O R C D
L R O Y G E T A R T S W E E
A K N D Y T E I C O S A V E
U I A D E D E F E C T S V F
Q N L S U O N E G O M O H E
Q G I S T S O C N E D D I H
```

Added	Fishbone	Measure	Scale
Benchmarking	Goal	Operational	Service
Cause	Graph	Party	Society
Costs	Hidden costs	Price	Standard
Culture	Homogenous	Process	Strategy
Cycle	Inspection	Product	Teamwork
Defects	Line	Quality circles	Time
E-Mail	Loss	Range	Value
Feedback	Means	Root	World class

3-3

Planning the Audit

D	A	E	L	U	D	E	H	C	S	D	R	O	C	E	R
A	P	C	E	N	E	S	E	O	N	A	L	P	H	S	E
P	U	L	A	T	S	S	T	S	E	T	U	Q	E	C	A
E	R	I	R	I	K	E	S	T	N	E	M	U	C	O	D
R	P	E	N	D	N	C	C	R	O	A	A	A	K	P	C
F	O	N	P	U	A	O	I	A	E	R	N	L	S	E	H
O	S	T	I	A	R	R	T	T	E	E	A	I	I	C	E
R	E	D	B	A	R	P	S	E	Z	V	G	T	T	N	C
M	R	R	D	A	T	A	I	G	I	I	E	Y	E	T	K
A	V	A	L	I	D	I	T	Y	S	E	M	A	I	L	L
N	K	D	O	L	T	R	A	I	N	W	E	I	C	A	I
C	O	N	T	R	O	L	T	D	O	W	N	M	H	M	S
E	O	A	S	E	L	A	S	K	T	N	T	F	A	C	T
O	B	T	T	A	P	H	A	S	E	M	I	T	N	N	O
F	I	S	E	N	O	I	T	A	Z	I	N	A	G	R	O
S	A	M	P	L	E	I	N	T	E	R	V	I	E	W	L

Audit	Fact	Preparation	Site
Book	Interview	Process	Size
Change	Lead	Purpose	Standard
Check	Learn	Quality	Statistics
Checklist	Link	Rank	Strategy
Client	Management	Rate	Step
Control	Name	Read	Task
Cost	Note	Records	Team
Data	Organization	Review	Test
Date	Performance	Sales	Time
Desk	Phase	Sample	Tool
Documents	Plan	Schedule	Train
E-Mail	Plot	Scope	Validity

59

3-4

Auditor

```
D O C U M E N T S A E N O M C
R P H H S P U W O L L O F A H
O E E F A C T C E P S N I E E
C N L I L R G S O C I C N T C
E I U P O M T E I R T O D N K
R N D R M E A N Q S E N I O L
A G E C E A A I U C G F N I I
V E H L I L S M A I N O G T S
A S C O P E N A L H I R S A T
D O S S T A E X I T T M R D N
N P O I R D D E T E E A E I E
E R D N A N A L Y Z E N P L I
G U E G C E T O O R M C O A L
A P S E E R A C A U S E R V C
D A K S O S W E I V R E T N I
```

Agenda	Desk	Lead	Report
Analyze	Documents	Mean	Root
Audit	Ethics	Meeting	Sample
Cause	Examine	Nonconformance	Schedule
Chart	Exit	Opening	Scope
Checklist	Fact	Plan	Site
Client	Findings	Purpose	Team
Closing	Follow-up	Quality	Trace
Data	Interview	Record	Validation

3-5

The Stakeholder

```
N  O  I  T  C  A  E  V  I  T  C  E  R  R  O  C
P  R  O  F  I  T  S  R  E  S  R  E  D  O  M  U
E  S  E  R  V  I  C  E  L  H  S  E  I  O  A  S
V  S  G  N  I  T  E  E  M  I  F  O  N  T  N  T
I  N  D  U  S  T  R  Y  S  P  U  I  L  C  U  O
T  O  T  A  L  A  G  T  K  R  T  O  I  A  A  M
C  D  N  E  E  I  R  R  B  O  U  N  C  U  L  E
E  R  E  F  A  A  O  A  R  C  R  C  K  S  I  R
F  O  M  L  R  W  W  I  T  E  E  A  N  E  P  E
F  C  E  A  A  M  N  N  E  S  S  E  N  I  L  I
E  E  G  E  T  G  L  I  S  S  C  O  D  O  A  L
T  R  A  D  E  O  W  N  L  O  O  T  O  M  N  P
S  A  N  D  E  S  I  G  N  U  R  P  S  E  O  P
O  O  A  Y  T  I  L  A  U  Q  T  E  A  M  T  U
C  O  M  P  L  I  A  N  C  E  S  L  A  O  G  S
```

Access	Future	Memo	Root
Cause	Goals	Monitoring	Service
Compliance	Grow	Pain	Ship
Corrective action	Industry	Plan	Supplier
Cost effective	Line	Process	Team
Customer	Loop	Profits	Tool
Deal	Loss	Quality	Total
Design	Management	Rate	Trade
Escorts	Manual	Record	Training
Fear	Meetings	Redo	Work

63

PART 4
Discover the Quality Quote

The next set of puzzles are like a quality quote treasure hunt in that they have famous quality quotes hidden in them. Solve the puzzle by hunting down and circling the hidden words of the quality quote. The author's name(s) is also hidden in the matrix. Circle the entire word of the quote, although many letters are used more than once and words usually overlap each other. These words may be forward, backward, up, down, as well as diagonally up and down and backward or forward.

In the formation of the matrix, additional words may have been formed that have nothing to do with the word puzzles. If a word is repeated in the quote, it is repeated in the puzzle. Words such a "a" "to" "is" "on" may be repeated in the puzzle and any one is correct; however, in the answer grid only one will be used.

4-1

Continuous Improvement

A	C	W	T	D	R	A	H	B	E	G
C	G	H	O	S	T	B	R	E	A	K
O	N	J	W	H	E	R	E	T	R	T
U	O	Y	N	A	P	V	O	W	H	O
L	S	I	S	F	R	I	N	E	Y	E
D	X	R	E	Y	O	U	D	E	D	Q
O	W	I	N	E	B	I	O	N	E	D
G	O	O	D	N	L	N	A	Y	A	I
Y	N	N	C	O	E	B	M	J	R	E
E	R	E	H	W	M	A	T	T	E	R
E	C	N	A	T	S	I	Y	D	N	A

"A problem is the distance between where you are now and where you could be—no matter how good you are now."

—Townsend and Gebhardt (Patrick L. Townsend and Joan E. Gebhardt)

67

4-2

Tunnel Vision

```
T O P G Y U D B W R N T U S R Y G O
Y U E B C L E N U N A B L E M J I C
R I P G R C K T V S X Z A U K T N L
A I A P A R E N M D I B H R L E C A
N Z C U Y V L I G O K N E E O L A N
N Y S V K B J D W R O M E A S U P I
Y E E M W R S E M L R F I S A P A G
L F I B Y T I R O J A M A O S R B I
A K A B U H D A R T J M V N O M L R
S R C N K E E N F O C K U R L E E O
T F Z H R Y A D A R T D M V R H V N
O F W N T O L E H T H O U G H T O F
```

"The majority of business men are incapable of original thought bcause they are unable to escape from the tyranny of reason."

—Ogilvy (David Ogilvy)

4-3

All Roads Lead to Rome

```
Q  U  T  O  W  N  S  E  N  D  E  R  E  V  E  W  O  H
U  Q  A  L  M  O  P  C  A  I  N  E  N  D  N  A  F  N
A  B  S  T  R  A  C  T  A  F  R  A  Z  A  D  I  O  R
L  O  N  E  Y  T  A  T  N  E  C  E  C  S  I  I  O  Y
I  N  K  S  K  G  N  H  O  G  V  G  I  Y  S  Y  D  L
T  H  E  F  J  E  Y  G  O  E  R  E  U  U  A  O  B  R
Y  H  L  P  Y  H  A  I  N  V  E  E  F  O  G  R  W  I
A  G  E  J  A  D  K  A  W  K  M  N  W  O  R  I  C  A
F  M  V  K  A  U  I  R  L  L  O  X  C  I  E  A  M  F
L  D  E  E  T  W  O  T  A  C  R  Y  R  L  E  B  U  S
I  D  L  H  Q  B  A  S  I  C  D  O  O  R  M  O  S  T
N  O  I  T  A  T  N  E  M  E  L  P  M  I  E  A  Q  O
G  E  B  H  A  R  D  T  I  V  E  U  W  S  N  I  J  N
S  H  D  R  A  W  R  O  F  F  R  L  L  A  T  H  E  M
```

"Quality in the abstract is fairly straightforward. Implementation, however, can lead to confusion and disagreement at even the most basic level."

—Townsend and Gebhardt (Patrick L. Townsend and Joan E. Gebhardt)

4-4

Mountaintop Experience

```
T H E S G G Y A U M S A G R E A T
R O L H L I S I F O A N N O V J H
O Y L T T N E M O M K L I F E R E
T H E S T I F E I L D O D E R F K
M W Y M L R G W O R L D N A Y H P
X E E V E N R A H A N N A S L R T
N C R Q A R A L P H I A M P E E S
L I S D R Y S D I E X I M P T W V
Y R D L H N D O O M U C O G O O F
Q F W V A S T W N O J G C R K L R
P O M N E N T H U S I A S M H E U
Z C D W R K N O P T V R S B F B P
F N Y K J D O A S I H P M U I R T
```

"Every great and commanding moment in the annals of the world is the triumph of some enthusiasm."

—Ralph Waldo Emerson

4-5

What Real Teams Do!

```
D  W  S  Y  A  W  O  H  C  V  B  N  M
I  A  N  N  Y  O  C  R  Y  U  I  O  P
S  L  D  E  N  A  N  S  M  I  T  H  M
T  A  K  I  E  R  V  O  R  N  H  A  E
I  U  B  A  S  O  G  A  T  Z  E  L  T
N  D  E  L  T  E  A  M  S  J  R  B  U
C  I  A  W  I  Z  L  E  D  I  E  K  B
T  V  I  A  M  I  E  N  D  L  B  R  I
I  I  N  Y  Y  E  R  N  E  W  Y  Q  R
O  D  D  S  T  F  I  G  B  L  B  G  T
N  N  I  K  H  F  D  R  R  A  A  P  N
S  I  T  A  S  N  L  O  I  E  C  Y  O
S  M  N  I  A  G  R  F  O  R  K  H  C
```

"Real teams always find ways for each individual to contribute and thereby gain distinction."
—Katzenbach and Smith (John Katzenbach and Douglas Smith)

4-6

Costs of Quality

A	L	L	E	H	T	C	O	E
R	T	G	H	E	A	O	U	V
E	B	A	N	M	H	S	N	L
G	T	C	H	I	W	T	Q	O
E	H	T	O	T	O	S	U	V
F	E	I	N	H	H	D	A	N
I	B	O	O	V	N	G	L	I
R	K	N	S	B	O	J	I	S
S	Q	S	G	N	I	H	T	R
T	U	C	R	O	S	B	Y	K
A	Y	E	N	O	M	A	M	S

"What costs money are the unquality things—all the actions that involve not doing jobs right the first time."

—Crosby (Philip Crosby)

77

4-7

Cooperation

A	R	T	T	U	O	H	G	U	O	R	H	T	S
S	C	G	H	A	B	R	O	L	N	C	H	E	K
E	P	O	N	N	O	I	S	I	C	E	D	L	I
C	R	I	O	U	F	I	G	I	O	N	E	L	L
N	O	G	P	R	F	A	U	I	M	O	V	I	L
E	D	O	R	I	D	S	S	B	P	B	E	K	F
R	U	G	O	O	E	I	S	M	A	D	I	E	U
E	C	E	C	D	A	I	N	E	N	T	H	R	L
F	T	C	E	M	N	O	M	A	Y	A	C	T	L
F	I	E	S	U	P	H	O	N	T	R	A	L	Y
I	V	Y	S	H	O	U	L	D	D	I	A	N	B
D	E	K	E	S	L	F	G	H	W	Q	O	G	D
L	H	Z	S	O	E	F	R	M	A	K	I	N	G

"Coordination and productive use of differences should be achieved by group decision making processes used skillfully throughout the company."

—Likert (Rensis Likert)

4-8

What Tomorrow Brings

Y	T	I	R	U	T	U	F	D	D	B	M	N
O	S	H	O	R	T	M	R	E	T	R	O	W
T	H	R	O	U	G	H	I	C	H	T	I	P
H	O	R	W	R	A	T	E	I	E	B	H	J
I	R	R	E	S	P	O	N	S	I	B	L	E
N	K	E	S	T	O	A	D	I	R	S	I	R
K	O	T	T	A	Q	U	M	O	E	L	L	A
S	N	E	R	F	O	P	I	N	T	O	N	E
Z	O	L	I	A	A	V	I	S	E	D	I	L
D	A	E	D	C	H	T	F	I	Y	O	N	P
Q	U	O	T	G	N	O	L	A	S	T	E	G
R	H	B	N	L	O	N	S	A	V	O	C	M
O	H	C	A	B	N	E	K	R	E	H	C	S

"Not to think through the futurity of short term decisions and their impact long after 'we are dead' is irresponsible."

—Scherkenbach (William Scherkenbach)

PART 5

Crazy Crosswords

The following set of puzzles are *Crazy Quality Daffynitions*. The answers are words from quality glossaries, but the clues to the puzzle are words that may have very different meanings (daffynitions) than you are used to. You will probably have to stretch your imagination a bit . . . so relax and have fun with them.

Quality Word List

The following words are provided to help make the link between the daffynition and the quality words easier. Refer to them if you're having trouble with the clues.

Acceptance sampling	Disposition
Added value	Downtime
Audit	Feedback
Benchmark	Fishbone
CARs	E-mail
Cause and effect	Goals
Checklist	Hidden costs
Collection	ISO
Consumer	Line
Control	Loop
Control limits	Lot plot
Culture	Mean
Data	Measurement
Default	Nonconformance
Detection	Operation

Policy
Process
Quality
Quality circles
Random
Range
Rank
Rate
Record
Review
Risk
Roadmap
Root
Root cause
Service
Size
Society
Statistics
Teamwork
Train
User
World class
Worst case
Writing

Crazy Quality Daffynitions

ACROSS
1. Cowboy's home
3. Cut or flat
5. Computer service
6. Not yielding to peer pressure
9. Star Trek II Commander
10. Gym socks past 3 days
11. One in a million or a ___ House Publication

DOWN
1. Atlas fame
2. What dogs do in a park
4. Out of control vacuum cleaner
7. Regurgitation
8. Carrot

Crazy Quality Daffynitions

ACROSS
2. ___ cheese food
5. Graveyard unit
7. Bull Mikey's aims
8. Can have 3 kinds of parties
10. International lecture
12. One of the 3 Rs
13. A bottom or telephone
14. Put on the line

DOWN
1. Oxen pull
3. Reason for carrots
4. Skewed circle
6. Autos
9. A morning-after need
11. Agar base occupant

Crazy Quality Daffynitions

ACROSS
1. Drug addict
3. Something to march in
5. A bite of mom's apple pie
9. Prefix with thermal or bar
10. Monroe's 36-26-36
11. Factoids
12. No tears for Crosby about it

DOWN
2. Partner with lies and damned lies
3. 45 RPM
4. Seafood lover's bane
5. Whipped cream or gravy
6. Church plate or grouping of dust
7. U.S. Foreign ____
8. Followers of John Birch

Crazy Quality Daffynitions

ACROSS
2. A kind of scenario
6. Worthy rounds
9. Footballer Joe Green's moniker
10. One for all (kind of)
11. Star Trek II commander
12. Goes with room or silver
14. Miss Marple's venue
15. May be sunny or gloomy

DOWN
1. Weekend papers' hunt
3. What Santa does twice
4. Karma
5. A "little one" could
7. Prevaricator's tool
8. $$ in small print
13. Gee as opposed to Haw

5-5
Crazy Quality Daffynitions

If you missed a clue the first time, you may have another chance in this puzzle.

ACROSS
2. $
3. Cowboys' home
5. Morning-after need
7. Karma
10. One for all
12. Goes with flat or cut
13. Regurgitation
14. May be 45 or 78 RPM
15. What dogs do in a park

DOWN
1. Weekend papers' hunt
2. Agar plate resident
3. Gym socks past 3 days
4. Bull Mikey's aims
6. Prevaricator's tool
8. Seafood lovers' bane
9. What Santa does twice
11. Oxen pull
16. Autos

PART 6

Quality Anecdotes

In this section of the puzzle book, you are invited to test your acuity at finding the quality errors. These are real situations, but names have not been included to avoid embarrassment. Put on your Sherlock Holmes (or is it quality auditor) cap and have fun with your evaluations.

Read the anecdote and answer the questions at the end of each story. Compare your response to the answers in the back of the book or, if you are in a classroom environment, with those of others responding to the same situation.

The following are statements describing the focus of each anecdote. You may select an anecdote in order to test yourself or simply start with the first one and work through to the end. You will be asked to identify the quality-related problems and to respond in a manner that promotes continuous quality improvement.

6-1: Fly-by-Night
The story describes a service situation in which things are not going as planned, and you are asked to identify customer interaction quality errors.

6-2: Ask the Customer
The story describes a situation in which the quality manager sets out to identify customer needs, only to meet a lot of resistance. You are asked to assess the situation and make a decision.

6-3: Making Impressions
The story describes an airline rebooking service. You are asked to identify actions that create both positive and negative impressions on the customer.

6-4: Moving Target
The story describes a situation requiring you to take actions that could have ethical implications.

6-5: Shipping Gone Haywire
The story describes a new quality project initiative, but the results don't show any improvement. You are asked to assess management's actions in response to the poor results.

6-6: Monopoly Potholes in Customer Service
The story describes a situation in which an organization (in a limited competitive environment) follows all its procedures but the customer is still unhappy. You are asked to identify why the customer may not be happy and how the situation may be different in a more competitive environment.

6-7: Making Suggestions
The story describes a situation in which a customer makes suggestions for improvement and how the service organization responds. You are asked to assess the actions by the service organization and the customer.

6-8: Handling a Complaint
In the story, you are given a customer complaint and asked to respond.

6-9: Quality First
The story describes a situation in which the quality manager is asked to do (accomplish) more than resources allow. You are asked to respond to upper management.

6-10: Regrade for Quality
The story describes a situation in which you achieve quality improvement (productivity and profit improvement), but management responds in an unexpected manner. You are asked to respond to management's actions.

6-1

Fly-by-Night

You board the plane twenty minutes before the scheduled departure time. At the departure time, the pilot announces that there will be about an hour delay. The delay is a result of having to wait for a mechanic to clear a hydraulic trouble light. There is no mechanic at this airport because the airline has contract maintenance at a nearby airport that houses the mechanics. The pilot explains that the hydraulic system trouble light had come on when he left the hub airport and that he had called ahead for a mechanic to meet the plane. However, the mechanic never received the original message and now it will take an hour for the mechanic to arrive. The pilot goes on to explain that the airplane hydraulic system received normal periodic maintenance at the hub airport and it is not unusual for the warning light to come on afterward. It should be a simple matter for the mechanic to verify that there is no hydraulic system problem and to clear the warning light. After the pilot's announcement, you check your flight schedule to affirm that you have only 1 hour and 10 minutes between your arrival at the hub and your connecting flight to your destination city.

Five minutes later you are able to deplane. You call the airline reservation service (they are helpful) and make alternative arrangements on another airline. However, you need to get your ticket back from the gate agent in order to rebook but now there are 30 people in line at the gate counter. Your alternate flight is leaving in 10 minutes, so you decide to go back through security (it is a small airport) to the ticket counter. The ticket counter area is empty except for three ticket agents. You explain your situation and that, if you could make this alternate flight, it would save their airline the cost of an overnight stay and make you a lot happier. The ticket agent said he couldn't leave the counter area . . . sorry. As you leave he turns back to the other two agents, who had nothing to do, to talk. You do not make the alternate flight.

An hour after the scheduled departure, the mechanic arrives. The gate agent announces that you will be departing in 5 minutes.

(Note: The airplane has about 200 seats and is 90 percent filled, which means that the 5-minute departure estimate is not reasonably obtainable.) Everyone lines up quickly to reboard the plane (you still hope that it will be possible to make the connecting flight). Thirty minutes later (an hour and a half behind schedule) everyone is reseated and you are ready for take-off, but alas, now there is no way that you will make your connecting flight.

Question(s):
How many quality errors/omissions can you detect in this scenario? You should have at least five.

1.

2.

3.

4.

5.

6.

6-2
Ask the Customer

You have been in sales for 20 years and have been able to meet your sales goals almost every year except during a couple of recession years in the middle of your career. You just attended a sales meeting where the quality manager said everyone must ensure that customer needs/requirements are being met. Your first reaction was that they didn't think you had been doing your job for the last 20 years. The quality manger provided some product specifications and said these are the parameters we test for and the ranges we can meet, so go to the customer and find out what they need. You thought the quality manager was crazy. All your customers are happy, so why open up a can of worms? Most of the time our product (Dew Drops) meets a set of typical properties/characteristics listed in our brochure, and we are proud that our product is the wettest in the industry (our Dew Drops have both the highest purity and highest water content).

The quality manager said he did not want a wish list, but specific customer needs. Future sales literature will contain specific Dew Drop specifications that we guarantee to our customer, and there will be no typical properties list.

Before going out on this self-destruct mission, you double-check with the sales manager to ensure that this is what is wanted. Armed with your new guaranteed purity specification you visit your first three customers on day one. Customer A says he needs consistent-sized Dew Drops, and wants a Dew Drops diameter specification. The next customer (Customer B) wants to be able to purchase very fine-sized Dew Drops from time to time so that the product can be used as a mist. Customer C states that she doesn't care anything about Dew Drops purity but would like what she called "dry" Dew Drops. The purchase manager goes on to say that operations is pushing for dryer Dew Drops, and she got some literature from another supplier who claims to have both dryer and wetter Dew Drops.

You find a phone and make a panic call to the sales manager. You tell him you may lose all three of the customers and want to know if you should contact other customers or put this initiative on hold. He tells you to call the quality manager to let him know what is going on.

Question(s):

As the quality manager what should you do? For example:

1. Stop the program until you have a better plan and can assess the effect on sales. Then explain.

2. Tell the sales person that this is exactly the information we need to know. Then explain some possible actions (short term and long term) as a result of the three customer concerns/needs.

3. Another response.

6-3

Making Impressions

Your plane arrives at the hub airport 15 minutes too late to make your connecting flight. You are met at your gate and told to go to the airline customer service counter to make alternate arrangements. There were three agents and one person being helped when you arrived at the customer service counter. Five minutes later there were three agents and 35 people in line wanting help. The agent who was helping you yelled out a couple of times over the next five minutes that there was another customer service counter 10 gates away and then grumbled to you about how stupid they (the passengers/customers) were for not going to the other gate. Trying to be agreeable you say, "It looks like you might need some additional help." The agent looked at you and said that she had "a break coming up in 10 minutes and was going to take it!" Finally, one of the other agents left the counter to explain to those in line about the other service counter. You notice that about 12 people left for the other counter. You then remark to the agent, "It looks like several people left for the other counter." Two agents responded that "No, hardly anyone went to the other counter," and that "People are just plain . . . well, you know what I mean."

Your two alternate flights for that evening were already overbooked and you end up with a voucher for a free night's stay and another for a $10 dinner. You have an 8:30 A.M. meeting the next day and the new flight will not arrive until 9:15 A.M. You inform the agent that you will need your luggage—to retrieve some important papers and clothes for tomorrow's meeting as well as your overnight bag. The agent says that your bags have been taken to the morning flight location and asks if you would like a complimentary overnight kit. You decline the overnight kit because you need your luggage with your suit for tomorrow morning's meeting. The agent makes the arrangements for you to pick up your baggage. Overall, the agent has been efficient at her job and seems very friendly. The agent ends the conversation with, "Have a nice day."

You arrive at the designated baggage claim area (reserved for special packages, odd sizes, and special circumstances) approximately 45 minutes after your arrival at the hub airport. As you wait and wait for your baggage, you watch various types of golf clubs, odd-size boxes, and mangled boxes marked "fragile" go by. Almost an hour later, your baggage pops up from the conveyor belt, unharmed except for being a little waterlogged. Apparently your baggage had been left out in the rain. No real harm is done except that your suit is a little damp.

Question(s):

1. What individual service personnel actions created a negative impression on you, the customer? (You should have at least five.)

2. What actions created a positive impression on you? (You should have at least three.)

6-4
Moving Target

Business has been slow, and finished product inventory has been building up. You are the quality control supervisor. Your boss comes back from a meeting with the general manager and states that incoming inspection needs to be tightened up by increasing the number of inspections and rejecting any orders that do not comply with 100 percent of the company's requirements. You are told that it is time to get tough on the suppliers to see who is serious about doing business with the company. Currently, you are following agreed upon sampling plans that are meeting production needs.

In your heart you believe that the new management direction is a ploy to reduce incoming material inventory without having to renege on promises to suppliers. Plus, if there is a shortage of raw materials and the production slowed down, the suppliers could be blamed. What should you do?

Question(s):

1. Are there any ethical issues in this situation?

2. Should you refuse to change the sampling plans and acceptance levels?

3. Should you notify the suppliers of the changes?

4. What are the options for dealing with this situation?

6-5
Shipping Gone Haywire

Everyone at the meeting was disappointed. The MIS department data showed that customer complaints regarding product distribution issues have steadily increased over the last four months. It was only six months ago that top management approved the overhaul and implementation of a continuous improvement program in the slow-to-change Distribution Department. As part of the program, the Distribution Department started ranking common carriers used by the company and vowed to drop poor performers. Other programs included:

- Upgrading dunnage and packing materials to ensure product is not damaged in transit.
- Shipping dock audits to improve accountability and to identify problem areas.
- Customer rights program to inform customers what they should expect from shippers as well as whom they should contact if shippers don't meet their expectations.

The Distribution Department has received a lot recognition over the last several months on some of their innovative approaches.

Three days ago, the vice president and general manager asked the MIS department to put together some data to assess the improvement of Distribution Department services for a performance review meeting. Now it appears that the changes have increased customer dissatisfaction to an all-time high. The data presented showed not only increased customer complaints but also a slight reduction in on-time delivery. The complaint information supplied by the MIS department was a surprise to the distribution manager and he was not able to adequately explain the situation to the general manager.

Four weeks after the performance review meeting, the distribution manager was transferred outside the headquarters facility to a lesser job at another facility.

Question(s):

What would you do? Was it time to bring in new blood and set things right?

Monopoly Potholes in Customer Service

Your spouse was on the telephone taking an important call when the door bell rang . . . ding dong, ding dong. Your spouse put down the phone and went to answer the door. It was a power company representative. The power company representative said that he was here to collect last month's bill of $154.34 or he was going to shut the power off right now. He was either going to leave with the money or turn off the power. Needless to say your spouse interrupted the important call and wrote out a check (thank goodness they would accept personal checks) to the power company. When you returned home from your business trip, your spouse related the story to you and asked how you missed paying the power bill. The problem with this scenario is that you had paid the bill on time (three weeks ago). You knew this to be true because you have electronic banking and $154.34 was transferred from your bank account to the power company's bank account. Actually, you had received a notice about a week after the bill was due that the power company was going to terminate your service due to failure to pay. Since you knew that the power company had your money, you assumed that the funds were posted late, and you would wait until next month's bill to see if the issue persisted. Little did you know that in three short weeks the power company would show up to turn your power off . . . completely.

You called the power company to complain, but no one had a record of the first payment. You did not have a canceled check (since the funds were transferred electronically), but you did have a bank statement showing the transfer. No one could help you, and you were basically treated as a delinquent payee. It was recommended that you go the power company Customer Service Center 30 miles away. At the Customer Service Center you stood in line at one of the four teller booths for people waiting to pay a bill or to make partial payments on past bills. When you approached the booth and the teller asked how much you were paying, you told her that you were here to collect money owed to you by the power company. This seemed to unsettle her at first, but she pulled up your file and then give you the same answer . . . there is no record of a payment (except the one collected at your home). Next, you were sent to a customer service representative. After a short wait you entered the customer service representative's office. You related your story again and showed her your proof of payment. She left and returned to explain that there was no record of payment and nothing the power could do without a canceled check. Then you explained to her that, from your view, you had proof that $154.34 had been transferred from your bank account to the power company, that the power company had your money, and you weren't leaving until they paid you what was due. She left to get a supervisor.

As you waited in the office you noticed a company quality policy and two awards for outstanding customer service. For some reason, you did not believe that you were getting the outstanding customer service referred to in the awards.

The story ended 45 minutes later when the supervisor found your payment in the records. You had inadvertently changed a 4 to a 7 in your nine-digit account number, and the power company had placed the money in a general fund. You got your money—but the story doesn't end just yet. You had to stay even longer to provide the information necessary to change your credit rating. It turns out that, even though you have paid utilities bills on time for 30 years, the power company submitted a report to the credit bureau that you were a bad credit risk. The supervisor submitted new information to cancel out the "late payee" report. As you left, the representative of the power company reminded you that this could have been avoided if you had not made the account number error.

Question(s):

1. Even though the utility company followed all its procedures, why would the customer still be unhappy?

2. What would this scenario look like in a competitive market (offering a choice of utility companies)?

6-7

Making Suggestions

You called the catalog sales company to check on the status of a special order. When you finished, you remarked to the warehouse service person that you would like to provide some customer feedback. The person on the other end of the line seemed confused at first, but then agreed to hear the information.

The feedback was that you were generally pleased with the service and items that you have purchased from the catalog company, but you have had a couple of recurring problems over the last three years. One problem was that, when you ordered items the day after receipt of the special sales catalog, they were already out of inventory. The company representative response was either that it shouldn't have happened or that you must have called in long after the new catalog came out.

The second issue was that you get two, and in some cases three, mailings of the same catalogs. The company representative confidently responded that "the computer did it." Further questioning of the customer service representative only resulted in "everyone does it that way."

Question(s):

1. What did the customer service representative do wrong?

2. What did the customer do wrong?

3. Why don't organizations listen unless there is a formal complaint?

6-8

Handling a Complaint

The following complaint letter was sent to the general manager of a major hotel chain. What would be your response to the complaint letter?

General Manager   October 22, 1997

RE: Room 1612 stay the evening of Oct. 21.

Dear General Manager,

I thought that the people at the hotel were delightful and very helpful. The accommodations were luxurious. However, I believe that there is room for some improvement in consistently meeting guest room requirements.

I encountered several problems with the basic amenities with the room itself. They are:

1. The toilet bowl was not cleaned from the prior guest. It looked like dried human waste had lined the part of the bowl above the water level.
2. The stopper for the bathroom sink did not hold water.
3. There were no coffee bags to make coffee in the machine.
4. Even if I were able to make coffee, there was no regular powdered cream.
5. The shampoo was not sealed. This is a personal thing...I always worry about using shampoo from an unsealed container for fear that someone has added something to it.
6. The stool (brown covered seat) in the bathroom had coffee stains on the cover.
7. There were no telephone instructions for how to dial out. Should one start with an "8" or "9"?

8. There was no summary of hotel facilities, restaurants, health club, etc.
9. The little TV in the bathroom had very poor reception. I would suggest that either the units be made more functional or they be eliminated.
10. The bathroom door sticks. If you enter the bathroom and close the door you cannot get out. It appears that the door locks, but in reality it only sticks. If you push down on the handle as you are pushing outward, the door will open.

If this is to be a world-class quality hotel, all service details need to be addressed. The above items did not seem to fit the otherwise excellent service by the staff.

Thank you for listening.

I.M. Customer

Question(s):

1. What points would you want to make in your response to the customer? For the actual response see page 178.

6-9

Quality First

You just received a promotion to the newly created position of director of quality. You believe that part of the reason you were given the promotion is your knowledge of the customers' quality criteria and your science background. In last month's meeting, the boss said he would like you to introduce the use of statistical tools in the workplace. Based on what he was told (and you confirmed), he believes that the scrap levels can be cut in half and save the company a lot of money. At this month's meeting, the boss indicates that he would like to achieve the highest rating, based on the customers' criteria. The customers' criteria are very similar to ISO 9001, and you don't see a problem except it would take about 18 months to add the necessary controls and to be ready for a customer qualification audit. And, by the way, your company is putting the finishing touches on a major acquisition.

Your staff consists of yourself, an assistant with quality engineering experience, a secretary, and a Claims/Complaint Department of eight people. There are five business units, each with its own quality assurance manager whom you normally work through. No additional staff is budgeted to be added in the next 12 months, and, if anything, the company is looking for opportunities to cut personnel. You have already been scheduled to participate for a week next month, as one of the pre-takeover evaluation team members for the major acquisition. You are worried that you may not be able to accomplish everything the boss wants. You don't want the to boss to think you can't do the job, and it may be politically incorrect to ask for more resources at this time. When you confided in a quality-consultant friend, she said you will not be able to do any of the jobs right and will make everyone unhappy.

Question(s):

1. What should you do?

6-10

Regrade for Quality

You have worked hard over the last 18 months since accepting your current position with the company. It has been a lateral move in terms of grade level, but it represented an opportunity for future advancement in management. Over the last 18 months you have taken some risks that were successful: You implemented a continuous quality improvement (preventive style of management), and your changes have resulted in a more efficient operation. Improvements allowed for both a staff reduction and 30 percent decrease in budget requirements. Upper management is very pleased, and you have been asked to take on additional duties so that you can work your magic there, too.

Earlier this week, the human resources director asked to meet with you. Your boss has not said anything, and you don't know what this could be about . . . maybe a promotion?

You get to the meeting and the human resources director explains the Bay's job rating system and how all jobs in the company are rated, which determines appropriate pay ranges. The HR director goes on to explain that, since there has been a reduction in your supervisory responsibilities and a lower department budget, your pay grade is being lowered. He says not to worry, that you will not need to take a pay cut, but future raises could be at a lower percentage since you will be at the top of the pay range. You are shocked, in disbelief, and you stammer through a couple of questions. Then the meeting ends.

Question(s):

1. What should you do?

2. Is the Bay's job rating system conflicting with quality improvement principles and overall objectives of the organization? If so, how could it be fixed?

PART 7

Find the Missing Word of the Quality Quote

The following puzzles are a step level up from Part 4 (the quality quote treasure hunt). All of these puzzles are missing a key word. To solve this puzzle, find the words of the quality quote in the diagram and deduce the one that is missing. The authors' names are also hidden in the diagram. Circle the entire word of the quote, because many letters are used more than once and words usually overlap each other. These words may be forward, backward, up, down, and diagonally up and down, backward, or forward. Then deduce the missing word from the quote given. Note: Words with fewer than five letters are never the missing ones. If a word is repeated in the quote, it is repeated in the puzzle.

In the formation of the matrix, additional words may have been formed that have nothing to with the word puzzles. Words with few letters (e.g., "a" "is" "on" "to," etc.) may be repeated in the puzzle, and any selection is correct; however, only one will be used in the answer grid.

7-1

Living in the Past

Find the missing word by circling the words of the following quote in the grid above.

"When an institution, organization, or nation loses its capacity to inspire high individual performance, its great days are over."

—Gardner (John W. Gardner)

Answer: _____

7-2

Top Down

A	Q	W	E	T	O	P	T	Y	U	I	O	P	D	F	J	W	H
M	N	D	R	Y	U	K	V	B	R	T	E	Y	E	S	I	H	G
V	S	X	N	B	C	B	D	K	J	U	Y	T	D	T	G	L	Y
E	V	I	M	D	S	N	D	F	H	K	L	R	H	U	D	F	W
B	E	N	H	W	A	S	E	T	U	I	N	O	X	T	X	D	C
B	S	C	C	V	N	V	Y	H	K	T	U	P	W	T	A	K	E
Z	X	O	R	S	O	U	I	S	D	T	H	P	K	A	L	O	P
P	F	M	I	A	Q	W	X	D	C	N	N	U	M	L	L	I	W
T	H	E	X	C	F	V	Q	E	O	T	Y	S	U	I	K	S	B
U	D	F	F	O	G	F	K	B	P	W	O	I	L	U	Y	T	R
P	M	S	R	Z	W	Q	O	D	T	Y	U	K	I	M	Z	E	X
A	H	M	O	D	F	D	G	M	L	O	P	U	N	E	W	H	Q
X	P	W	M	N	Y	K	E	H	T	N	E	M	E	T	A	T	S

Find the missing word by circling the words of the following quote in the grid above.

"Nobody will take his eyes off the income statement or put his heart on the line without support from the top."

—Davidow and Uttal (William Davidow and Bro Uttal)

Answer: _____

7-3

Bottom Line

```
T  Q  W  R  E  S  T  F  G  R  Y  T  I  L  A  U  Q
I  H  K  I  S  H  X  M  E  S  U  J  S  D  N  J  K
X  F  A  S  K  J  R  M  D  J  V  B  N  M  D  A  R
Q  W  R  T  D  R  O  A  Z  U  X  C  E  M  H  K  Y
T  H  E  C  B  T  F  J  G  D  K  T  L  L  S  E  T
Q  W  E  R  S  D  F  G  D  G  V  H  X  Z  Y  N  M
W  E  R  U  U  I  O  P  D  E  V  E  I  H  C  A  L
S  C  C  V  B  N  M  J  K  S  R  D  B  W  E  T  S
O  A  L  L  A  N  V  A  S  H  G  N  N  M  C  K  P
B  N  O  N  M  I  C  V  B  S  R  E  H  T  E  H  W
```

Find the missing word by circling the words of the following quote in the grid above.

"In the end, it is the customer that judges whether quality and fitness for use are achieved."
—Allan Sayle

Answer: _____

7-4

Problem Solved

```
C  E  M  U  K  H  D  R  T  H  O  S  E  P
S  A  F  G  H  J  E  L  I  H  O  M  R  D
A  S  U  C  C  E  E  D  E  B  A  O  A  S
A  J  M  S  U  C  C  E  E  D  B  T  O  H
V  H  A  L  E  N  U  C  U  L  E  K  L  J
B  L  N  D  N  A  S  U  E  X  V  B  W  L
S  E  I  W  S  A  N  M  L  S  C  H  L  Y
E  A  B  O  H  C  S  D  O  L  O  R  O  A
S  O  N  E  S  O  H  T  E  W  Q  H  R  B
P  Y  T  I  L  A  U  Q  O  F  M  G  T  M
Z  A  C  V  X  B  R  T  Y  U  F  A  N  P
O  M  I  K  L  U  F  E  S  U  M  E  O  W
A  N  T  N  I  A  Q  W  P  O  R  K  C  Q
G  N  I  K  A  M  S  F  G  M  T  A  H  T
```

Find the missing word by circling the words of the following quote in the grid above.

"It may be said that those who succeed in problem-solving in quality control are those who succeed in making a useful cause and effect diagram."

—Kume (Hitoshi Kume)

Answer: _____

125

7-5

Majority of One

Find the missing word by circling the words of the following quote in the grid above.

"Despite what the textbooks say, most important decisions, in corporate life, are made by individuals, not committees."

—Iacocca (Lee Iacocca)

Answer: _____

Whose Job Is It Anyway?

```
N O I T A R T S I N I M D A
O E F T R U L Y S D R Q K L
T N F A X S N M K T S U O J
R G A Q W E V X F Z Y A K E
S I M E C N I V O R P L V Q
L N X F N O W R R T G I R U
G E P L O Y X D N M S T E A
S E C I V R E S F U G Y T L
L R A T H E V U L A I M T I
E I T O K V X C S L T H A T
P N O R M E X E L W S B M Y
O G N I T E K R A M W B O J
```

Find the missing word by circling the words of the following quote in the grid above.

"Quality is not the exclusive province of engineering, manufacturing, or for that matter services, marketing or administration. Quality is for everyone."

—Opel (John R. Opel)

Answer: _____

7-7

What's Happening?

E	S	E	S	E	H	C	T	A	M
X	I	R	A	P	S	A	U	G	A
P	S	U	Q	N	O	W	H	A	T
E	W	O	R	Y	H	O	W	Q	C
C	H	Y	E	E	K	Y	O	U	H
T	A	I	N	T	O	O	S	A	E
A	T	S	W	H	A	T	U	L	S
T	I	N	P	D	O	S	M	I	O
I	R	T	C	M	H	G	I	T	S
O	O	P	E	E	R	U	O	Y	T
N	D	R	O	W	H	E	N	O	A
S	S	N	E	P	P	A	H	U	H
S	H	A	P	P	E	N	S	S	W

Find the missing word by circling the words of the following quote in the grid above.

"Quality is not what happens when what you do matches your intentions, it is what happens when what you do matches your customer's expectations."

—Guaspari (John Guaspari)

Answer: _____

131

"I Love Ya' Tomorrow" (Annie)

```
A  F  W  T  S  U  J  A  L  A  T
C  H  I  L  D  G  N  I  O  D  Q
P  A  L  C  O  D  K  E  C  O  U
W  R  L  O  A  E  S  L  L  E  A
F  R  M  M  G  N  I  T  M  S  L
S  I  N  E  T  K  T  F  N  N  I
T  N  T  L  E  L  S  E  S  T  T
A  G  I  S  Z  X  P  U  I  T  Y
H  T  R  O  W  P  J  O  S  S  O
T  O  N  P  A  O  L  Y  O  U  R
G  N  I  H  T  Y  N  A  L  J  M
```

Find the missing word by circling the words of the following quote in the grid above.

"Quality like anything else worth doing, doesn't just happen. It's not like tomorrow, you just can't wait and it will come to you."

—Harrington (H. James Harrington)

Answer: _____

7-9

Train to Nowhere!

Find the missing word by circling the words of the following quote in the grid above.

"If your company's leaders are merely passengers, no one will drive you anywhere and Total Quality Management will not even be on your map."

—George (Steven George)

Answer: _____

7-10

What's for Dessert?

A	S	G	N	I	H	T	H	E	Y
S	E	C	I	D	U	J	E	R	P
I	V	L	S	S	I	A	C	R	U
S	O	G	I	T	T	I	O	F	D
H	T	I	W	I	F	O	N	P	D
I	H	S	N	L	F	Y	T	A	I
K	E	G	O	L	T	N	R	E	N
A	R	E	A	I	Q	A	O	R	G
W	E	L	L	V	C	M	L	E	T
A	G	A	I	N	S	T	K	H	H
T	U	B	M	I	F	G	O	T	E
Q	E	H	T	N	U	O	M	A	M

Find the missing word by circling the words of the following quote in the grid above.

"As with many other things, there is a surprising amount of prejudice against quality control, but the proof of the pudding is still in the eating."

—Ishikawa (Kaoru Ishikawa)

Answer: _____

137

Final Puzzle

Stands Alone

JP and Jan both find this quote by Norman Mailer so awesome that we decided to end this book with it.

ACROSS
4. Combines with either
5. For ___ record
7. Majority of ___
8. ___ and order
10. A compliance/standard word
11. Opposite of here
14. Identical
15. ___ what?
18. Pro
19. A kind of dirt
21. Ordered

DOWN
1. One of 6 "W"s for interviewing
2. Shelf ___
3. Evolve
5. Opposite of this
6. Other
9. The "J" in J.I.T.
12. Leftover
13. No longer is
14. ___ there!
16. One ___ these days
17. ___ and unusual
20. A joiner
22. Smallest article

Fill in your answers on the next page!

Find the Missing Word of the Quality Quote

_____ _____ _____
_____ _____ _____
_____ _____ , _____
_____ _____ , _____
_____ _____ _____
_____ _____ _____
_____ _____ _____
_____ _____ _____ .

—Norman Mailer

Answer Section

Quality Crossword Quotes

1-1: Go to the Source

"To find out how to improve productivity, quality, and performance, ask the people who do the work."

—*Harvard Business Review*

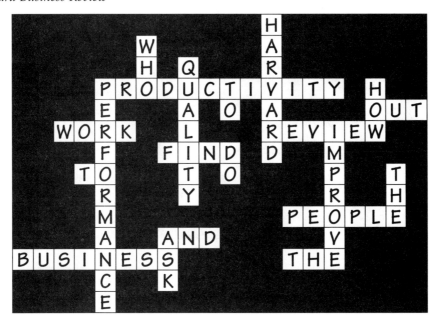

1-2: Expense vs. Benefit

"Quality is the degree of excellence at an acceptable price and the control of variablity at an acceptable cost."

—Robert A. Broh

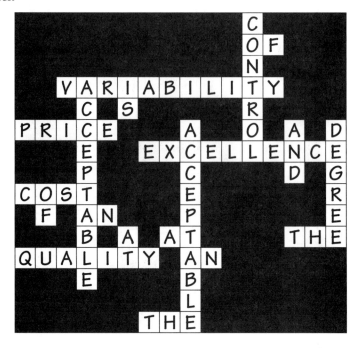

1-3: The Struggle

"The tone and fiber of our society depend upon a pervasive, almost universal striving for good performance."

—John W. Gardner

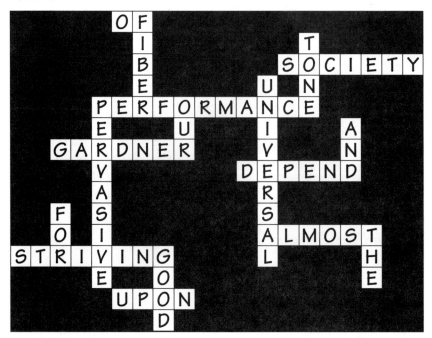

1-4: Anarchy

"A committee is a group of the unwilling chosen from the unfit to do the unnecessary."

—Anonymous

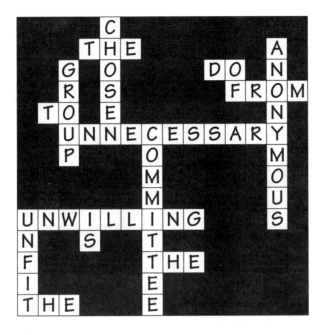

1-5: The Success Duo

"People and quality are the vital link to success in the twenty-first century."

—J. P. Russell

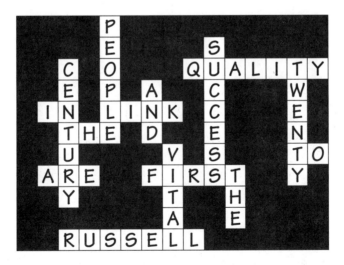

1-6: Lost at Sea

"We cannot have islands of excellence in a sea of slovenly indifference to standards."

—John W. Gardner

1-7: In a Class by Itself

"If you have world class quality products, services, and people, you will also generate world class profits."

—V. Daniel Hunt

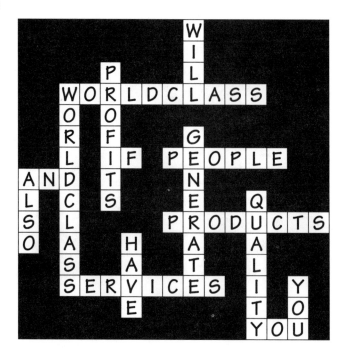

1-8: How Do We Get There?

"The future cannot be secured by technology, by new promotional campaigns, or just by working harder."

—J. P. Russell

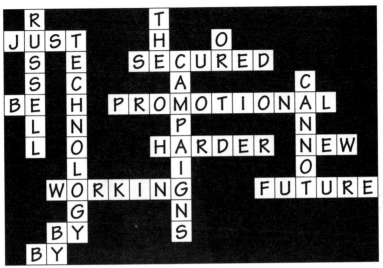

1-9: Molehills Not Mountains

"All problems become smaller if, instead of indulging them, you confront them."

—William S. Halsey

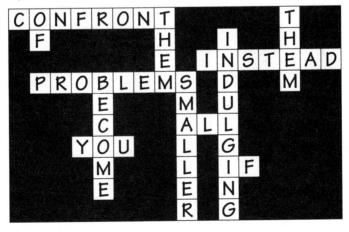

1-10: Mind and Matter

"Quality depends on good data. It also depends on executive leadership."

—Juran Institute, Inc.

1-11: Magic of Discovery

"The magic of employee involvement is that it allows individuals to discover their own potential."

—Philip Caldwell

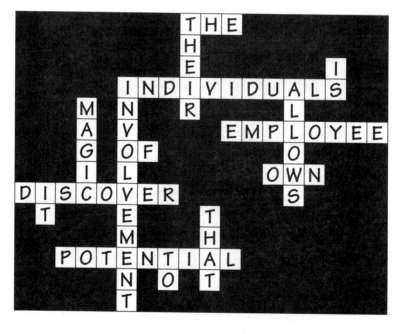

1-12: Mental Overload

"The biggest problem facing American business today is that most managers have too much information."

—Lee Iacocca

1-13: The Educated Eye

"The ability to treat matters from the statistical viewpoint is more important than the individual methods."

—Hitoshi Kume

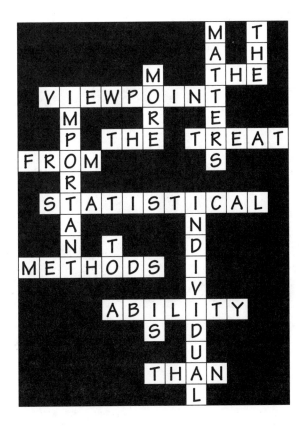

1-14: The Key to It All

"Customers are the most important asset any company has, even though they don't show up on the balance sheet."

—Thomas Berry

1-15: "Make It So" (Captain Jean Luc Picard)

"To achieve improvement at a revolutionary pace, requires that improvement be made mandatory."

—J. M. Juran

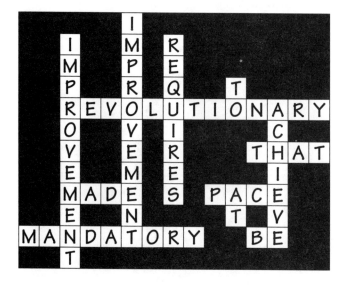

1-16: Hit and Run

"It is not sufficient to implement a solution and walk away from it. This could do more harm than good."

—J. P. Russell and Terry Regel

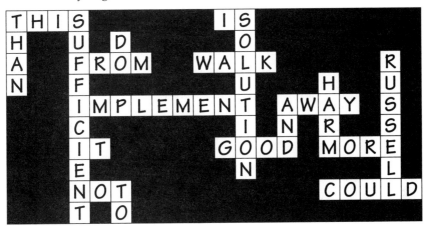

Coded Quality Quotes

2-1: Just Reward
"If you do what you've always done, you'll get what you've always gotten."

—Anonymous

2-2: Poor Vision
"It isn't that they can't see the solution. It is that they can't see the problem."

—G. K. Chesterton

2-3: Astounding!
"If we all did the things we are capable of doing, we would literally astound ourselves."

—Thomas Edison

2-4: How's Your Aim?
"If TQM is aimed at anything, it is aimed at winning and keeping customers."

—Thomas Berry

2-5: Make Change
"If change is to occur, it must come about through hard work within the organization itself."

—Gordon Lippitt

2-6: Prime Importance
"It is the first of all problems for a man to find what kind of work he is to do in this universe."

—Thomas Carlyle

2-7: Oh to Joy!
"It is a joy to have the benefit of what is good, it is a greater one to experience what is better."

—Goethe

2-8: We Aim to Please
"High quality means pleasing customers not just protecting them from annoyances."

—David Garvin

2-9: Go for the High Road
"Any time you sincerely want to make a change, the first thing you must do is to raise your standards."

—Anthony Robbins

2-10: The Prevaricator's Tool

"There are three kinds of lies: Lies, damn lies, and statistics."

—Mark Twain

2-11: A Word to the Wise

"Probabilities direct the conduct of the wise man."

—Cicero

2-12: What Makes It Tick?

"When it comes to making the place run, motivation is everything."

—Lee Iacocca

2-13: The Ugly!

"The worst thing a person can do is to ignore or cover up a problem."

—Masaaki Imai

2-14: Look for the Silver Lining

"An optimist sees an opportunity in every calamity; a pessimist sees a calamity in every opportunity."

—Anonymous

2-15: Well, I Reckon

"It is in general more profitable to reckon up our defects than to boast of our attainment."

—Thomas Carlyle

2-16: Pass the Word On

"You want people praising to others about owning your product or service, not just complaining."

—William Scherkenbach

Find the Quality Words

3-1: In the Field

```
V  N  N  O  I  T  A  C  I  F  I  C  E  P  S
A  G  I  R  L  E  H  B  I  A  T  O  N  L  S
L  I  A  E  O  E  R  N  U  C  E  S  I  A  A
U  S  R  Z  C  A  D  R  Y  T  M  T  L  N  L
E  E  T  K  N  I  P  R  O  C  E  D  U  R  E
A  D  N  G  N  R  D  Q  F  R  I  E  Z  I  S
D  E  E  G  O  E  G  U  I  D  E  L  I  N  E
D  T  M  D  F  O  R  A  E  E  C  L  O  S  E
E  E  U  E  F  A  I  L  L  S  C  O  O  P  Y
D  C  C  F  I  E  C  I  D  E  A  A  L  E  T
T  T  O  A  S  Y  S  T  E  M  S  A  R  C  S
I  N  D  U  S  T  R  Y  E  I  N  R  A  T  E
G  O  A  L  U  U  L  O  R  T  N  O  C  A  T
H  C  T  T  E  F  U  N  C  T  I  O  N  E  A
T  C  A  E  R  F  L  O  W  D  E  T  A  I  L
```

3-2: Quality Business

```
T E R A P W D R A D N A T S
F I S H B O N E C Y C L E S
D E D D A R V C E M A I L Q
W O R K M L A I R S E M I T
S T R U N D L V U I O N C E
E T H T T C U R S T S O C H
L R O C I L E E A P A R T Y
C B O U C A U S E H P A R G
R E P D I S O C M E A N S T
I N E O E S T E A M W O R K
C C R R G I S S E C O R P C
Y H A P O F F L E G N A R A
T M T N A G M E N I L O I B
I A I D L E L A C S O R C D
L R O Y G E T A R T S W E E
A K N D Y T E I C O S A V E
U I A D E D E F E C T S V F
Q N L S U O N E G O M O H E
Q G I S T S O C N E D D I H
```

156

3-3: Planning the Audit

D	A	E	L	U	D	E	H	C	S	D	R	O	C	E	R
A	P	C	E	N	E	S	E	O	N	A	L	P	H	S	E
P	U	L	A	T	S	S	T	S	E	T	U	Q	E	C	A
E	R	I	R	I	K	E	S	T	N	E	M	U	C	O	D
R	P	E	N	D	N	C	C	R	O	A	A	A	K	P	C
F	O	N	P	U	A	O	I	A	E	R	N	L	S	E	H
O	S	T	I	A	R	R	T	T	E	E	A	I	I	C	E
R	E	D	B	A	R	P	S	E	Z	V	G	T	T	N	C
M	R	R	D	A	T	A	I	G	I	I	E	Y	E	T	K
A	V	A	L	I	D	I	T	Y	S	E	M	A	I	L	L
N	K	D	O	L	T	R	A	I	N	W	E	I	C	A	I
C	O	N	T	R	O	L	T	D	O	W	N	M	H	M	S
E	O	A	S	E	L	A	S	K	T	N	T	F	A	C	T
O	B	T	T	A	P	H	A	S	E	M	I	T	N	N	O
F	I	S	E	N	O	I	T	A	Z	I	N	A	G	R	O
S	A	M	P	L	E	I	N	T	E	R	V	I	E	W	L

3-4: Auditor

```
D O C U M E N T S A E N O M C
R P H S P U W O L L O F A H
O E E F A C T C E P S N I E E
C N L I L R G S O C I D C C
E I U P O M T E I R T O E K
R N D R M E A N Q S E N T L
A G E C E A A I U C G F I I
V E H L I S M A I N O O S
A S C O P E N A L H I R T S
D O S S T A E X I T T M R A T
N P O I R D D E T E E R D N
E R D N A N A L Y Z E N P I E
G U E G C E T O O R M C O L
A P S E E R A C A U S E R V L
D A K S O S W E I V R E T N I
```

3-5: The Stakeholder

```
N  O  I  T  C  A  E  V  I  T  C  E  R  R  O  C
P  R  O  F  I  T  S  R  E  S  R  E  D  O  M  U
E  S  E  R  V  I  C  E  L  H  S  E  I  O  A  S
V  S  G  N  I  T  E  E  M  I  F  O  N  T  N  T
I  N  D  U  S  T  R  Y  S  P  U  I  L  C  U  O
T  O  T  A  L  A  G  T  K  R  T  O  I  A  A  M
C  D  N  E  E  I  R  R  B  O  U  N  C  U  L  E
E  R  E  F  A  A  O  A  R  C  R  C  K  S  I  R
F  O  M  L  R  W  W  I  T  E  E  A  N  E  P  E
F  C  E  A  A  M  N  E  S  S  E  N  I  L  I
E  E  G  E  T  G  L  I  S  S  C  O  D  O  A  L
T  R  A  D  E  O  W  N  L  O  O  T  O  M  N  P
S  A  N  D  E  S  I  G  N  U  R  P  S  E  O  P
O  O  A  Y  T  I  L  A  U  Q  T  E  A  M  T  U
C  O  M  P  L  I  A  N  C  E  S  L  A  O  G  S
```

Discover the Quality Quote

4-1: Continuous Improvement

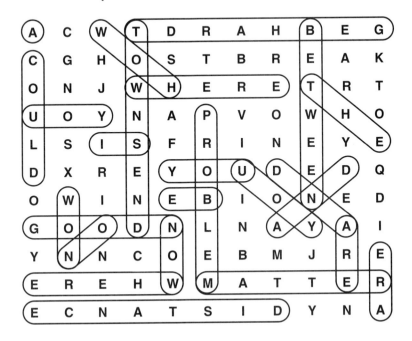

"A 'problem' is the distance between where you are now and where you could be—no matter how good you are now."

—Townsend and Gebhardt (Patrick L. Townsend and Joan E. Gebhardt)

4-2: Tunnel Vision

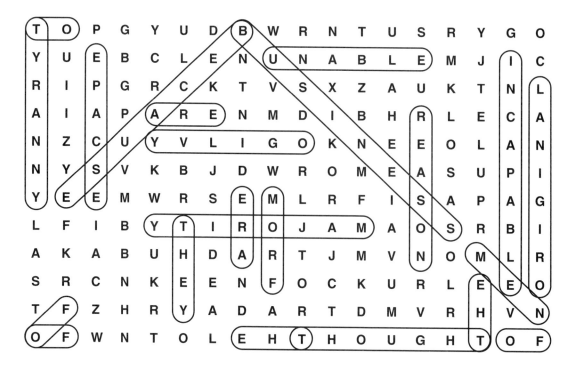

"The majority of business men are incapable of original thought because they are unable to escape from the tyranny of reason."

—Ogilvy (David Ogilvy)

4-3: All Roads Lead to Rome

"Quality in the abstract is fairly straightforward. Implementation, however, can lead to confusion and disagreement at even the most basic level."

—Townsend and Gebhardt (Patrick L. Townsend and Joan E. Gebhardt)

4-4: Mountaintop Experience

```
T H E  S  G  G  Y  A  U  M  S  A  G  R  E  A  T
R O L  H  L  I  S  I  F  O  A  N  N  O  V  J  H
O Y L  T  T  N  E  M  O  M  K  L  I  F  E  R  E
T H E  S  T  I  F  E  I  L  D  O  D  E  R  F  K
M W Y  M  L  R  G  W  O  R  L  D  N  A  Y  H  P
X E E  V  N  R  A  H  A  N  N  A  S  L  R  T
N C R  Q  R  A  L  P  H  I  A  M  P  E  E  S
L I S  D  R  Y  S  D  I  E  X  I  M  P  T  W  V
Y R D  L  H  N  D  O  O  M  U  C  O  G  O  O  F
Q F W  V  A  S  T  W  N  O  J  G  C  R  K  L  R
P O M  N  E  N  T  H  U  S  I  A  S  M  H  E  U
Z C D  W  R  K  N  O  P  T  V  R  S  B  F  B  P
F N Y  K  J  D  O  A  S  I  H  P  M  U  I  R  T
```

"Every great and commanding moment in the annals of the world is the triumph of some enthusiasm."

—Ralph Waldo Emerson

4-5: What Real Teams Do!

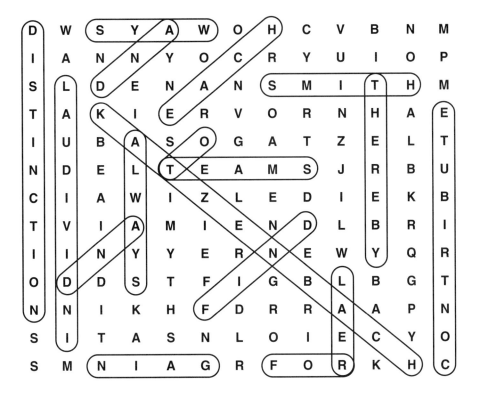

"Real teams always find ways for each individual to contribute and thereby gain distinction."
—Katzenbach and Smith (John Katzenbach and Douglas Smith)

4-6: Costs of Quality

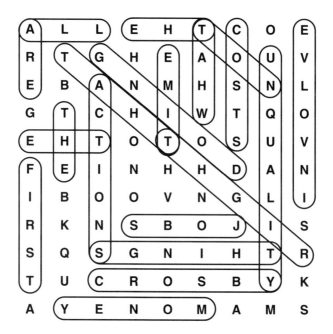

"What costs money are the unquality things—all the actions that involve not doing jobs right the first time."

—Crosby (Philip Crosby)

4-7: Cooperation

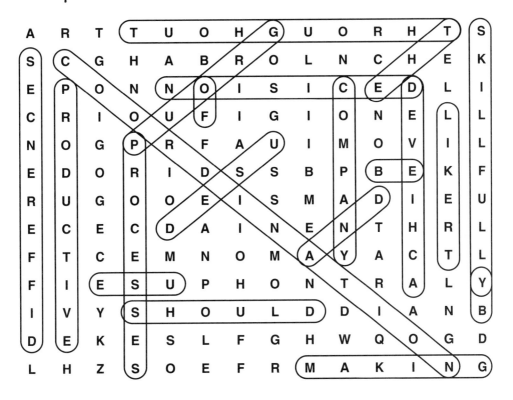

"Coordination and productive use of differences should be achieved by group decision making processes used skillfully throughout the company."

—Likert (Rensis Likert)

4-8: What Tomorrow Brings

"Not to think through the futurity of short term decisions and their impact long after 'we are dead' is irresponsible."

—Scherkenbach (William Scherkenbach)

Crazy Crosswords

5-1: Crazy Quality Daffynitions

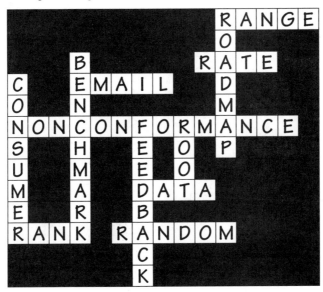

5-2: Crazy Quality Daffynitions

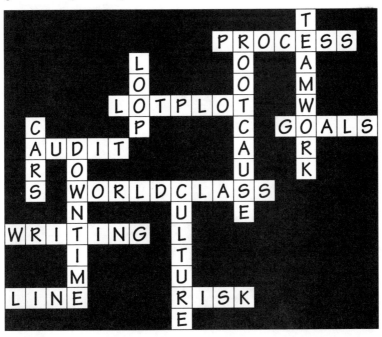

5-3: Crazy Quality Daffynitions

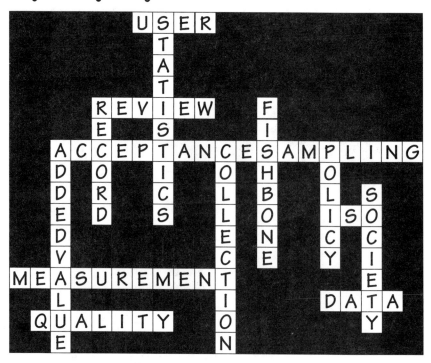

5-4: Crazy Quality Daffynitions

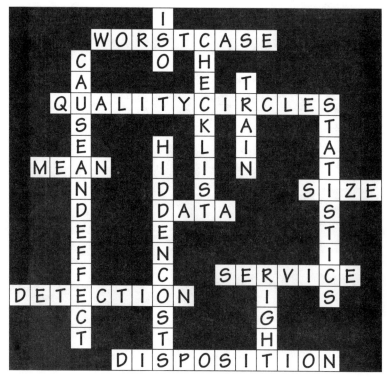

5-5: Crazy Quality Daffynitions

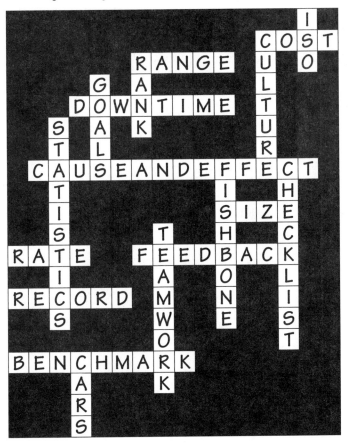

Quality Anecdotes

6-1: Fly-by-Night

The following represent some of the quality errors/omissions:

1. The plane was loaded although there was no mechanic to check and okay the aircraft.
2. The pilot waited until departure time to announce the delay.
3. The process of contacting the mechanic did not work.
4. The airline averted one problem at the hub through preventive maintenance on the hydraulic system but created another one by not following through.
5. The appearance of the warning light after the hydraulic system repair was a recurring problem known to pilots, but there was no apparent system to address it.
6. The ticket agent was not empowered to assess the situation and make small deviations from normal practice in order to meet customer needs (e.g., collect/verify the existing ticket and reissue).
7. After the repair, the gate agent actually created further customer dissatisfaction by raising expectations with the announcement that the plane would be loaded and ready to take off in 5 minutes.

6-2: Ask the Customer

Number 2 is the best answer, assuming you, as quality manager, did not jump the gun in the first place. To put things on hold would be very damaging to the quality initiative. Of course, it would have helped to better prepare the sales force so that they would know what to expect.

Responses:

Customer A: Find out what diameter works best for customer A. If sales needs support, it is okay for the quality manager or technical service representative to visit Customer A with the salesperson. In the short term it may be possible to sort Dew Drops by size and send the size the customer needs. In the long term, there needs be a program either to be able to make specific Dew Drops sizes to order, or to have a classification method (sort of the Dew Drops).

Customer B: The company is finding out that one size Dew Drops does not fit all applications. It may turn out that the sorting to satisfy Customer A will also meet Customer B needs for fine Dew Drops. This may be an opportunity for a new specialty product (fine Dew Drops) that could result in increased sales (new markets) and/or higher profit margins as a result of higher pricing for specialty products.

Customer C: The need for both wetter and dryer Dew Drops could pose a major technical problem and competitive threat (competition already offering dryer and wetter Dew Drops choices).

It may be appropriate for the development folks to be involved with meeting the customer requirements. Follow up with the customer to express your interest in working with her to design what she needs and secure competitive samples to determine how your product compares to the competition.

Other Responses:

There are several possible responses to the sales person's dilemma. However, in all cases the immediate customer concerns should be addressed. Long-term issues that affect production and technology should be identified to remain competitive in the marketplace.

6-3: Making Impressions

1. *What individual service personnel actions created a negative impression on the customer?*
    1. The agent's yelling at customers from behind the counter.
    2. The agent's telling a customer that other customers were stupid.
    3. The agent's telling a customer that, even though it was busy, she was going to take her break anyway.
    4. Airline personnel contradicting a customer over an issue that was not important to anyone (i.e., that several people left for the other counter).
    5. The seeming inappropriateness of the "Have a nice day" salutation.
    6. Baggage handlers' mishandling baggage.

2. *What actions created a positive impression on the customer?*
    1. Having someone meet the plane and direct passengers to the customer service counter.
    2. The agent who went out to speak to the passengers rather than yell at them from behind the counter.
    3. Efficient customer service personnel.
    4. Making arrangements for you to get your luggage so you didn't have to go to another service counter ("one stop shop" concept).

6-4: Moving Target

It is not unusual for management to use quality as a tool for punishment. It goes back to an original perception of quality as slowing things down and unnecessarily increasing costs. So why not use it against the suppliers to slow things down in the name of goodness (quality)?

1. *Are there any ethical issues in this situation?*

    The word *unethical* deals with failure to follow a code of conduct. Sometimes the code of conduct is not a written document but is a perception of how people should act in certain situations. Basically it refers to a moral duty or obligation not to intentionally lie or deceive. Since this example deals with the quality profession, we can refer to ASQ's code of conduct for conforming to acceptable professional standards. The elements of the code of conduct that may apply here are:

- You will be honest and impartial; will serve with devotion your employer, your clients, and the public.

- You will act in a professional manner as a faithful agent or trustee for each employer or client.

- You will indicate to your employer or client the adverse consequences to be expected if your professional judgment is overruled.

- You will not disclose information concerning the business affairs or technical processes of any present or former employer or client without his or her consent.

2. *Should you refuse to change the the sampling plans and acceptance levels?*

   It seems premature to refuse to change the sampling plans and acceptance levels at this point. The code of conduct does not imply that you should refuse to do work, only that if you are in disagreement, you should inform your employer of possible outcomes.

3. *Should you notify the suppliers of the changes?*

   If changes are made to the acceptance criteria and sampling plans it would be reasonable to notify the suppliers. It would also be both good business practice and ethical to notify them of any change in requirements.

4. *What are the options for dealing with this situation?*

   The first step would be to tell your boss that you will look into the possibilities of changing the acceptance criteria and assess the impact on the business. Next, identify the incoming materials that would be affected and review existing inspection data. Determine the cost of increasing the sampling confidence levels (e.g., from 3 sigma to 6 sigma), as well as of testing certified supplier materials (not currently tested) and the benefits to the organization. Identify increases in staffing requirements and/or the impact of dropping other projects your team is working on. In other words, view this as a serious request and do a professional job of evaluating and planning the implementation. Then go back to the boss with your report and recommendations. If the original sampling plans were well thought out it is unlikely that management will want to change them now, knowing all the facts. However, the new data may turn up areas to both increase and decrease inspection, so be flexible.

Author's Comment: It may turn out that the general manager will decide that comments to "tighten up on suppliers" were misunderstood. The point is that some requests from upper management may be vague or terminology may be used that is not in conformance with the terms normally used in the quality assurance field.

6-5: Shipping Gone Haywire

The answer from a project implementation view is that it was the wrong time to transfer the Distribution Department manager unless he was part of the cause of the problem. From a data information view, one must know the assumptions and in many cases see the raw data to identify anomalies.

In this case, the information was correct but management did not take into account an expected increase in customer complaints as a result of their aggressive customer rights program and the policy of classifying all customer dissatisfactions as customer complaints. Previously, only line item charges such as cost to return goods were classified as customer complaints.

Management must give careful thought before making changes during a project or new business initiative. The removal of the Distribution manager would be noticed and could send a couple of unofficial messages to the other managers/employees. The informal message could be that upper management expects results and if you don't produce you will be replaced, or (more important from a continuous quality improvement perspective) that it is dangerous to make changes and any risks should be avoided.

The problems in the Distribution Department already existed, but they were hidden from view. The quality initiative only highlighted the problems so that they could be addressed.

6-6: Monopoly Potholes in Customer Service

1. *Even though the utility company followed all its procedures, why would the customer still be unhappy?*

    First, the company showed up to cut off power service before adequately investigating the situation. Second, the customer was treated as if he was wrong, and no one (except the supervisor later on) was empowered or took the initiative to investigate further (assuming the customer is right). The final blow was to find out how swiftly the power company had initiated action to tarnish an individual's credit rating.

2. *What would this scenario look like in a competitive market (offering a choice of utility companies)?*

    In a competitive market (and/or quality-focused organization) the utility company would assume that the customer was telling the truth. Then the problem would have been simply to find out where the money had been credited.

This is just one symptom of how some companies, particularly monopolies and pseudo monopolies, don't understand customer service. They focus on internal standards (rule books) and give themselves awards for adhering to them—with little regard to customer satisfaction (needs).

The heavy-handed tactic of turning off the power was not called for. There were safety issues—the lack of heat, the use of unsafe alternate lighting sources at night, loss of use of the sewer facilities because the lift pump would no longer operate, and complicating emergency situations—that would need to be addressed in the absence of a power source.

In a competitive environment, the company would have to consider the potential loss of 20 years of power revenue ($150/month × 12 months × 20 years = $36,000) if it lost the customer, plus the possibility that if the company was in error, the individual would complain to others and even more customers could be lost.

In a more competitive environment, the company would realize that it is more economical to keep existing customers than to acquire new ones. Hence, the company would be more sensitive to customer satisfaction and service issues.

Author's Comment: A reviewer commented that I was making an unfair assumption that monopolies equal bad customer service. I am not suggesting that all monopolies and pseudo monopolies provide poor customer service. However, the story is true, and the reasons I chose it over others were my utter disbelief of what happened and the realization of the authority and power the utility company had over us.

6-7: Making Suggestions

1. *What did the customer service representative do wrong?*

    Refocusing for a moment, we can say that the customer representative didn't do anything wrong, it is management's fault. Apparently, the customer representative was not trained to accept suggestions for improvement. He was trained only to address item-by-item warehouse inquiries.

    A simple response would have been for the customer service representative to listen to the customer, make notes, and pass them on to the appropriate person or supervisor. The best solution is for organizations to set up methods for accepting and evaluating what could be called suggestions for improvement (being proactive) rather than only responding to errors and problems.

2. *What did the customer do wrong?*

    Once the customer realized there was no system for accepting comments or suggestions the matter should have been dropped—unless the complaint could have been rephrased in a form that required action for resolution.

3. *Why don't organizations listen unless there is a formal complaint?*

    Many organizations are just starting to listen to customer complaints and taking action to resolve them. The bottom line is that if a complaint does not require action on the part of the organization, many times the complaint becomes "nice to know" information only. It is a big step to admit that the customer is right some of the time, and it is more economical to keep good customers than to gain new ones.

    Many organizations are taking the next step (delighting customers), but there aren't as many of them as there should be.

Author's Comment: The point of this story is not centered on a catalog sales company, it is about making suggestions. Most companies are set up only to handle complaints that require action—not suggestions or ideas for improvement. Don't waste your time.

6-8: Handling a Complaint

(Key points are in *italics*.)

I.M. Customer

Any Town USA

Dear Mr. Customer:

Thank you for *taking the time* to write us regarding your stay on October 21. I want to *apologize for* the condition in which you found your room. There is *no excuse* for it. I want to assure you that the *matter has been addressed* with both our housekeeping manager as well as our director of engineering.

The DownTown Hotel *is the finest hotel* in the city, but in your case we obviously did not live up to our reputation. We can only hope that you will look upon this as an isolated incident and give us the *opportunity to serve you again.* In an effort to make amends, I would like to offer you a one-night complimentary stay at DownTown. Please contact the reservations manager, Sharon, when you are ready to secure your reservations.

On a positive note, I was *happy to read* that you found our staff to be quality individuals. Thank you.

Mr. Customer, if there is anything I can do for you in the future, please *do not hesitate to call* me. Again thank you for your letter, and I hope to hear from you soon.

Sincerely,

General Manager

Key Point Summary:
- Thanking the customer
- Apology
- No excuses
- Action taken
- Organization positives
- Come back and try us again
- Thanking for, and recognizing the positive points in, the complaint letter
- Open door

6-9: Quality First

1. *What should you do?*

   The situation is that it is impossible to do what the boss wants, even if you work seven days a week. But if you tell the boss you can't, it will sound like someone who is always telling people what they can't do, rather than what they can do.

   First, let us assume that you could accomplish everything that was requested if you had the resources. One approach would be to put together a plan to accomplish all the major objectives—acquisition support, implementation of customer criteria (ISO 9001), and start up of a statistical process control system. Once the plan is put together, decisions can be made concerning resources (people, capital), timing, and priorities.

   People resources can be supplemented by internal temporary transfers, assignment to external temp agencies, outsourcing specified tasks to consulting organizations, and hiring new employees. Other options are to change the scope of the projects (narrow them or implement them in phases), or extend the time line for completion.

   Committing to projects that you do not believe can be completed as planned is not in your best interests or your employer's. The allocation of resources is a business decision.

6-10: Regrade for Quality

1. *What should you do?*

   There is very little that an employee can do in this situation. Appealing to the boss is one option.

   In the actual situation, the employee appealed to the boss, which ultimately resulted in a transfer to another department. The boss was not able to convince the HR manager to maintain the employee's grade level in the current position.

2. *Is the Bay's job rating system conflicting with quality improvement principles and overall objectives of the organization? If so, how could it be fixed?*

   A compensation system that primarily rewards managers for head counts and the size of their department budgets does not promote quality improvement. Compensating factors must be added to encourage the employee to improve operations without fear of being a casualty.

   This is an example of management system control that, in certain situations, can be adverse to organizational objectives for improvement.

Find the Missing Word of the Quality Quote

7-1: Living in the Past

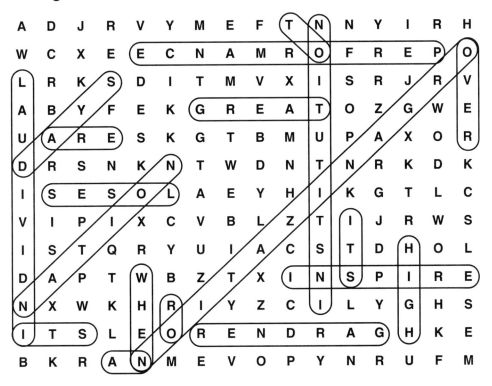

"When an institution, organization, or nation loses its capacity to inspire high individual performance, its great days are over."

—Gardner (John W. Gardner)

Answer: Capacity

7-2: Top Down

A	Q	W	E	T	O	P	T	Y	U	I	O	P	D	F	J	W	H
M	N	D	R	Y	U	K	V	B	R	T	E	Y	E	S	I	H	G
V	S	X	N	B	C	B	D	K	J	U	Y	T	D	T	G	L	Y
E	V	I	M	D	S	N	D	F	H	K	L	R	H	U	D	F	W
B	E	N	H	W	A	S	E	T	U	I	N	O	X	T	X	D	C
B	S	C	C	V	N	V	Y	H	K	T	U	P	W	T	A	K	E
Z	X	O	R	S	O	U	I	S	D	T	H	P	K	A	L	O	P
P	F	M	I	A	Q	W	X	D	C	N	N	U	M	L	L	I	W
T	H	E	X	C	F	V	Q	E	O	T	Y	S	U	I	K	S	B
U	D	F	F	O	G	F	K	B	P	W	O	I	L	U	Y	T	R
P	M	S	R	Z	W	Q	O	D	T	Y	U	K	I	M	Z	E	X
A	H	M	O	D	F	D	G	M	L	O	P	U	N	E	W	H	Q
X	P	W	M	N	Y	K	E	H	T	N	E	M	E	T	A	T	S

"Nobody will take his eyes off the income statement or put his heart on the line without support from the top."

—Davidow and Uttal (William Davidow and Bro Uttal)

Answer: Heart

182

7-3: Bottom Line

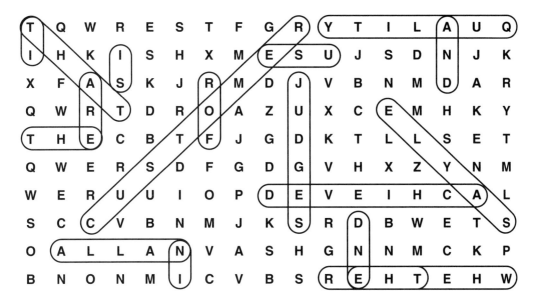

"In the end, it is the customer that judges whether quality and fitness for use are achieved."
—Allan Sayle

Answer: Fitness

7-4: Problem Solved

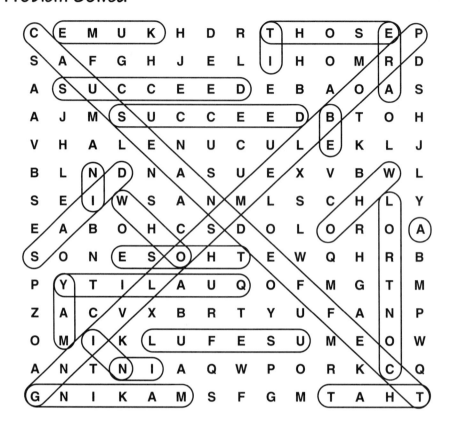

"It may be said that those who succeed in problem-solving in quality control are those who succeed in making a useful cause and effect diagram."

—Kume (Hitoshi Kume)

Answer: Diagram

7-5: Majority of One!

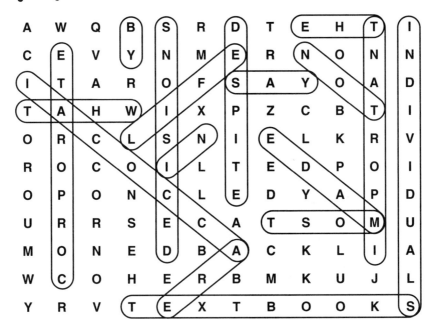

"Despite what the textbooks say, most important decisions, in corporate life, are made by individuals, not committees."

—Iacocca (Lee Iacocca)

Answer: Committees

7-6: Whose Job Is It Anyway?

"Quality is not the exclusive province of engineering, manufacturing, or for that matter services, marketing or administration. Quality is for everyone."

—Opel (John R. Opel)

Answer: Manufacturing

7-7: What's Happening?

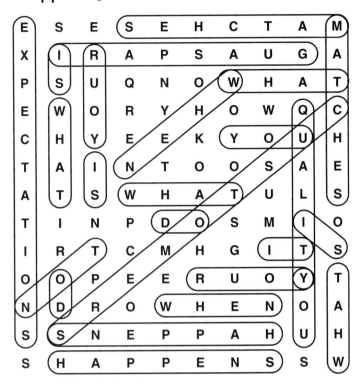

"Quality is not what happens when what you do matches your intentions, it is what happens when what you do matches your customer's expectations."

—Guaspari (John Guaspari)

Answer: Intentions

7-8: "I Love Ya' Tomorrow" (Annie)

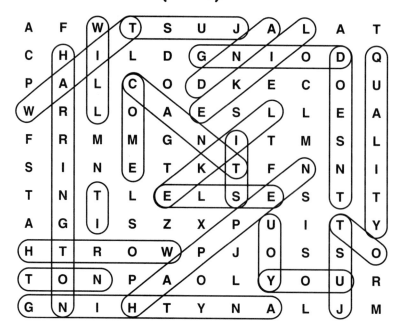

"Quality like anything else worth doing, doesn't just happen. It's not like tomorrow, you just can't wait and it will come to you."

—Harrington (H. James Harrington)

Answer: Tomorrow

7-9: Train to Nowhere!

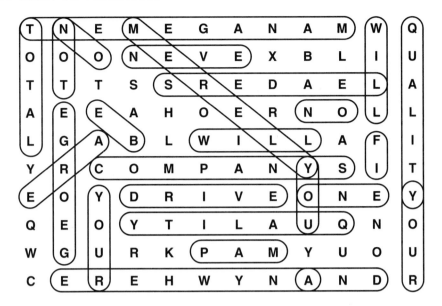

"If your company's leaders are merely passengers, no one will drive you anywhere and Total Quality Management will not even be on your map."

—George (Steven George)

Answer: Passengers

7-10: What's for Dessert?

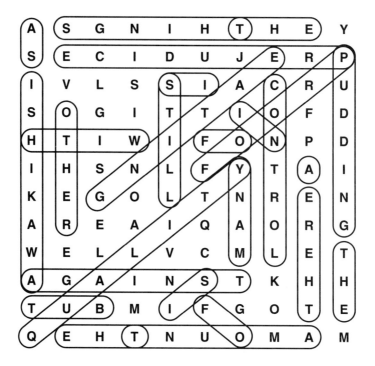

"As with many other things, there is a surprising amount of prejudice against quality control, but the proof of the pudding is still in the eating."

—Ishikawa (Kaoru Ishikawa)

Answer: Surprising

Final Puzzle: Stands Alone

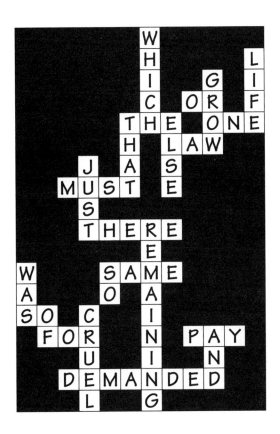

"There was a law of life so cruel, and so just, which demanded that one must grow or else pay for remaining the same."

—Norman Mailer

Source Reference List

Anonymous. Original source unknown, quoted in Helio Gomes, *Quality Quotes* (Milwaukee: ASQ Quality Press, 1997). "If you do what you've always done, you'll get what you've always gotten." p. 153.

Anonymous. "An optimist sees an opportunity in every calamity; a pessimist sees a calamity in every opportunity." p. 154.

Anonymous. "A committee is a group of the unwilling chosen from the unfit to do the unnecessary." p. 145.

Berry, Thomas. *Managing the Total Quality Transformation* (New York: McGraw-Hill, 1990). "If TQM is aimed at anything, it is aimed at winning and keeping customers." p. 153.

———. "Customers are the most important asset any company has, even though they don't show up on the balance sheet." p. 150.

Broh, Robert A. Original source unknown, quoted in Helio Gomes, *Quality Quotes* (Milwaukee: ASQ Quality Press, 1997). "Quality is the degree of excellence at an acceptable price and the control of variability at an acceptable cost." p. 144.

Caldwell, Philip. Original source unknown, quoted in Helio Gomes, *Quality Quotes* (Milwaukee: ASQ Quality Press, 1997). "The magic of employee involvement is that it allows individuals to discover their own potential." p. 148.

Carlyle, Thomas. Original source unknown, quoted in Helio Gomes, *Quality Quotes* (Milwaukee: ASQ Quality Press, 1997). "It is the first of all problems for a man to find what kind of work he is to do in this universe." p. 153.

———. "It is in general more profitable to reckon up our defects than to boast of our attainment." p. 154.

Chesterton, G. K. Original source unknown, quoted in Helio Gomes, *Quality Quotes* (Milwaukee: ASQ Quality Press, 1997). "It isn't that they can't see the solution. It is that they can't see the problem." p. 153.

Cicero. "Probabilities direct the conduct of the wise man." p. 154.

Crosby, Philip. *Quality Is Free: The Art of Making Quality Certain* (New York: Mentor, 1980). "What costs money are the unquality things—all the actions that involve not doing jobs right the first time." p. 166.

Davidow, William, and Bro Uttal. *Total Customer Service: The Ultimate Weapon* (New York: Harper Perennial, 1990). "Nobody will take his eyes off the income statement or put his heart on the line without support from the top." p. 182.

Edison, Thomas. Original source unknown, quoted in Helio Gomes, *Quality Quotes* (Milwaukee: ASQ Quality Press, 1990). "If we all did the things we are capable of doing, we would astound ourselves." p. 153.

Emerson, Ralph Waldo. Original source unknown, quoted in Helio Gomes, *Quality Quotes* (Milwaukee: ASQ Quality Press, 1990). "Every great and commanding moment in the annals of the world is the triumph of some enthusiasm." p. 164.

Gardner, John W. *Excellence* (New York: Norton, 1987). "The tone and fiber of our society depend upon a pervasive, almost universal striving for good performance." p. 144.

———. "We cannot have islands of excellence in a sea of slovenly indifference to standards." p. 146.

———. "When an institution, organization, or nation loses its capacity to inspire high individual performance, its great days are over." p. 181.

Garvin, David. Original source unknown, quoted from Helio Gomes, *Quality Quotes* (Milwaukee: ASQ Quality Press, 1997). "High quality means pleasing customers not just protecting them from annoyances." p. 153.

George, Steven. *The Baldrige Quality System: The Do-It-Yourself Way to Transform Your Business* (New York: John Wiley & Sons, 1992). "If your company's leaders are merely passengers, no one will drive you anywhere and Total Quality Management will not even be on your map." p. 189.

Goethe. Original source unknown, quoted in Helio Gomes, *Quality Quotes* (Milwaukee: ASQ Quality Press, 1997). "It is a joy to have the benefit of what is good, it is a greater one to experience what is better." p. 153.

Guaspari, John. *The Customer Connection: Quality for the Rest of Us* (New York: AMACOM, 1988). "Quality is not what happens when what you do matches your intentions, it is when what you do matches your customer's expectations." p. 187.

Halsey, William S. Original source unknown, quoted in Helio Gomes, *Quality Quotes* (Milwaukee: ASQ Quality Press, 1997). "All problems become smaller if, instead of indulging them, you confront them." p. 147.

Harrington, H. James. *The Improvement Process: How America's Leading Companies Improve Quality* (New York: McGraw-Hill, 1987). "Quality like everything else worth doing, doesn't just happen. It's not like tomorrow, you just can't wait and it will come to you." p. 188.

Harvard Business Review. Original source unknown, quoted in Helio Gomes, *Quality Quotes* (Milwaukee: ASQ Quality Press, 1997). "To find out how to improve productivity, quality, and performance, ask the people who do the work." p. 143.

Hunt, V. Daniel. *Managing Quality: Integrating Quality and Business Strategy* (Homewood, IL: Business One Irwin, 1993). "If you have world class quality products, services, and people, you will also generate world class profits." p. 146.

Iacocca, Lee. "The biggest problem facing American business today is that most managers have too much information." p. 149.

———. "Despite what the textbooks say, most important decisions, in corporate life, are made by individuals, not committees." p. 185.

Iacocca, Lee, and William Novak. *Iacocca: An Autobiography* (New York: Bantam Books, 1984). "When it comes to making the place run, motivation is everything." p. 154.

Imai, Masaaki. *Kaizen: The Key to Japan's Competitive Success* (New York: McGraw-Hill, 1996). "The worst thing a person can do is to ignore or cover up a problem." p. 154.

Ishikawa, Kaoru. *Introduction to Quality Control* (Tokyo: 3A Corporation, 1993). "As with many other things, there is a surprising amount of prejudice against quality control, but the proof of the pudding is still in the eating." p. 190.

Juran Institute, Inc. *Quality Benchmarks for Executives: Executive Planning Guide* (Wilton, CT: 1991). "Quality depends on good data. It also depends on executive leadership." p. 148.

Juran, J. M. *Made in the USA: A Break in the Clouds* (Washington, DC: Feb. 1990). "To achieve improvement at a revolutionary pace, requires that improvement be made mandatory." p. 150.

Katzenbach, John, and Douglas Smith. *The Wisdom of Teams: Creating the High-Performance Organization* (New York: Harper Business, 1994). "Real teams always find ways for each individual to contribute and thereby gain distinction." p. 165.

Kume, Hitoshi. *Statistical Methods for Quality Improvement* (Tokyo: Association for Overseas for Technical Scholarship, 1992). "The ability to treat matters from the statistical viewpoint is more important than the individual methods." p. 149.

———. "It may be said that those who succeed in problem-solving in quality control are those who succeed in making a useful cause and effect diagram." p. 184.

Likert, Rensis. *The Human Organization: It's Management and Value* (New York: McGraw-Hill, 1967). "Coordination and productive use of differences should be achieved by group decision making processes used skillfully throughout the company." p. 167.

Lippitt, Gordon. *Organizational Renewal: Achieving Viability in a Changing World* (Englewood Cliffs, NJ.: Prentice Hall, 1969). "If change is to occur, it must come about through hard work within the organization itself." p. 153.

Mailer, Norman. Original source unknown, quoted in J. P. Russell, *The Quality Master Plan* (Milwaukee: ASQ Quality Press, 1990). "There was a law of life so cruel, and so just, which demanded that one must grow or else pay for remaining the same." p. 191.

Ogilvy, David. *Confessions of an Advertising Man* (New York: Atheneum, 1980). "The majority of business men are incapable of original thought because they are unable to escape from the tyranny of reason." p. 162.

Opel, John R. Original source unknown, quoted in Helio Gomes, *Quality Quotes* (Milwaukee: ASQ Quality Press, 1997). "Quality is not the exclusive province of engineering, manufacturing, or for that matter services, marketing or administration. Quality is for everyone." p. 186.

Robbins, Anthony. *Awaken the Giant Within: How to Take Immediate Control of Your Mental, Emotional, Physical, and Financial Destiny!* (New York: Simon & Schuster, 1992). "Any time you sincerely want to make a change, the first thing you must do is to raise your standards." p. 153.

Russell, J. P. *The Quality Master Plan* (Milwaukee: ASQ Quality Press, 1990). "People and quality are the vital link to success in the twenty-first century." p. 145.

———. "The future cannot be secured by technology, by new promotional campaigns, or just by working harder." p. 147.

Russell, J. P, and Terry Regel. *After the Quality Audit: Closing the Loop on the Audit Process* (Milwaukee: ASQ Quality Press, 1996). "It is not sufficient to implement a solution and walk away from it. This could do more harm than good." p. 151.

Sayle, Allan. Source unknown, quoted in Helio Gomes, *Quality Quotes* (Milwaukee: ASQ Quality Press, 1997). "In the end, it is the customer that judges whether quality and fitness for use are achieved." p. 183.

Scherkenbach, William. *The Deming Route to Quality and Productivity: Road Maps and Roadblocks* (Washington, DC: CEEPress Books, 1990). "You want people praising to others about owning your product or service, not just complaining." p. 154.

———. "Not to think through the futurity of short term decisions and their impact long after 'we are dead' is irresponsible." p. 168.

Townsend, Patrick L., and Joan E. Gebhardt. *Quality in Action: 93 Lessons in Leadership, Participation, and Measurement* (New York: John Wiley & Sons, 1992). "A 'Problem' is the distance between where you are now and where you could be—no matter how good you are now." p. 161.

———. "Quality in the abstract is fairly straightforward. Implementation, however, can lead to confusion and disagreement at even the most basic level." p. 163.

Twain, Mark. "There are three kinds of lies: Lies, damn lies, and statistics." p. 154.